Globalization and Structural Change in the U.S. Forest Sector: An Evolving Context for Sustainable Forest Management

PETER INCE, ALBERT SCHULER, HENRY SPELTER, WILLIAM LUPPOLD

I0411753

*A Technical Document Supporting
the USDA Forest Service Interim Update of the 2000 RPA Assessment*

U.S. DEPARTMENT OF AGRICULTURE   FOREST SERVICE

Abstract

This report examines economic implications for sustainable forest management of globalization and related structural changes in the forest sector of the United States. Globalization has accelerated structural change in the U.S. forest sector, favored survival of larger and more capital-intensive enterprises, and altered historical patterns of resource use.

Keywords: globalization, structural change, forest sector, sustainability

Units of Measure

All dollar amounts are United States currency. Measurements in billions (10^9) use the U.S. system.

Cover photo: Toucan Arrow. Used by permission of Gearbulk Ltd, Surrey KT10 9EP, United Kingdom

March 2007

Ince, Peter; Schuler, Albert; Spelter, Henry; Luppold, William. Globalization and structural change in the U.S. forest sector: an evolving context for sustainable forest management. General Technical Report FPL-GTR-170. Madison, WI: U.S. Department of Agriculture, Forest Service, Forest Products Laboratory. 62 p.

A limited number of free copies of this publication are available to the public from the Forest Products Laboratory, One Gifford Pinchot Drive, Madison, WI 53726–2398. This publication is also available online at www.fpl.fs.fed.us. Laboratory publications are sent to hundreds of libraries in the United States and elsewhere.

The Forest Products Laboratory is maintained in cooperation with the University of Wisconsin.

Contents

Executive Summary

This report examines economic implications for sustainable forest management of globalization and related structural changes in the forest sector of the United States. The report covers a broad range of topics, but this summary focuses on three hypotheses.

One hypothesis is that economic globalization accelerated structural (largely irreversible) change in the overall economy and in forest product markets since the early 1990s, with exposure to import competition on a wider scale. Evidence for this hypothesis includes the following points.

Since the early 1990s, rapid expansion of goods imports and competition in export markets contributed to a recent downturn in U.S. industrial production (from 2000 to 2002). Import competition and loss of growth in exports quelled price inflation and reduced profits for U.S. manufacturers during that period. In that context, U.S. manufacturers were compelled to pursue production efficiencies and cost cutting more aggressively through structural changes, including productivity-enhancing technological changes, consolidation, outsourcing, and restrained capacity growth.

Acceleration of structural change was evidenced by nearly a tripling in the ongoing rate of labor displacement or productivity gains in U.S. manufacturing since the early 1990s, as goods imports tripled and the trade deficit expanded 10-fold. Structural change was evidenced also by the loss of historical correlation between U.S. industrial output and gross domestic product (GDP) growth over the past decade. After increasing for much of the previous century, U.S. output of forest products such as wood pulp and wood furniture also peaked in the past decade and then declined. Imports were the fastest growing component of softwood lumber and structural wood panel supply to U.S. markets.

By 2002, total U.S. timber harvest was estimated to be nearly 10% less than it was a decade earlier. With limited capacity growth, forest product markets exhibited cyclical volatility, but productivity gains and imports offset long-run inflationary pressures, and timber market volatility was relatively subdued in recent years with fairly adequate supplies and slower growth in demand. Current projections of future timber demand and prices are much lower than a decade ago (before the recent era of economic globalization and structural change in the forest sector).

A second hypothesis is that globalization and import competition favored survival of forest product enterprises in the United States that are more capital-intensive, less labor-intensive, and generally larger, more productive, and globally connected. Evidence for this hypothesis includes the following points.

The import share of U.S. consumption rose across the entire forest product sector in the past decade, but domestically produced shares of consumption remained higher for more capital-intensive and globally robust industries such as pulp and paper or structural wood panels, while falling to lower levels for less capital-intensive or more labor-intensive industries such as sawmills and furniture plants.

A commonly referenced business strategy was to develop customized products or to seek niche markets as a refuge from volatile global commodity markets, but average output capacities of lumber mills, pulp mills, and paper mills all increased and the number of mills declined, as smaller, less efficient mills were closed. Ongoing structural changes in computing, electronic communication, and product distribution accelerated the design, production, and delivery of goods, such that larger firms gained flexibility to rapidly exploit customized or niche market opportunities. Meanwhile, foreign firms or subsidiaries of multinational firms in other countries also obtained the means to quickly and efficiently develop customized products and exploit niche markets, as evidenced by expanded outsourcing of custom wood furniture production and expansion of U.S. wood furniture imports.

An implication of these trends is that markets for the primary product of forestry and forest management activities on private lands, namely timber, will be driven by future development (or lack of development) in larger scale forest-product enterprises that serve increasingly global markets. There is little evidence for the notion that globalization and structural change will lead to expansion of smaller scale forest enterprises. Instead, the focus on niche markets or customized products should be understood as a commercial strategy that is being pursued aggressively by larger globally oriented enterprises to develop branding, product identity, and product value in increasingly competitive global markets.

The last hypothesis is that economic globalization and ongoing structural changes altered familiar patterns of resource use, economic pathways, and opportunities to advance sustainable forest management in the United States. Evidence for this hypothesis includes the following points.

Structural changes stemming from economic globalization over the past decade included consolidation and realignment of production capacity in the interest of competitive cost savings in forest product manufacturing. Such changes have contributed recently to a notable decline in the real economic value of forestry outputs such as timber, as well as other measures such as forest sector employment, economic feasibility of forest management, and gross output of forestry (the contribution of forestry to U.S. GDP). Economic globalization and the structural trade deficit also made U.S. housing construction increasingly dependent on foreign purchases of U.S. financial assets.

All of these changes reflect deep impacts on the economic, social, and environmental context of forest management in the United States, suggesting that more in-depth strategic monitoring and analysis of economic globalization is warranted in planning sustainable forest management policies for the future, with careful consideration given to ways to cope with the challenges of globalization and structural change. For example, careful consideration needs to be given to what strategic approaches should concern forest managers and policy makers in this context, how those approaches will improve the opportunity for sustaining forests, and how structural changes will alter future management opportunities. To a large extent, the efficacy of different approaches will depend on their success in sustaining the global competitiveness of the U.S. forest sector.

Eight different categories of strategic approaches are identified that might be aimed at sustaining the global competitiveness of the U.S. forest sector, including (1) considering import duties, wage or benefit constraints, tax incentives, or subsidies; (2) promoting U.S. environmental and labor standards globally; (3) liberalizing trade; (4) achieving free currency exchange; (5) gaining in automation, efficiency, and productivity; (6) developing global enterprise; (7) promoting product differentiation and certification; and (8) advancing the resource and technology infrastructure as well as training and skills needed for future sustainable forest sector development. All of these strategic approaches have limitations or drawbacks. Without more detailed analysis, there is little basis for speculation about the effects of the strategies on the competitiveness of the U.S. forest sector, and it would be misleading to suggest that any particular approach is recommended. However, a mix of these approaches is already being pursued to some extent; thus, understanding consequences of globalization and structural change for sustainable forest management will require monitoring and evaluating a spectrum of behavioral responses and forest management options that will unfold in the evolving context of forest sector globalization, consolidation, and structural change.

Following is a summary of important points about economic globalization and structural change that were derived from this report and that appeared also in the Interim Update of the Resources Planning Act (RPA) Assessment (USDA Forest Service 2007).

There is a long history of structural change in the U.S. forest products industries as timber harvesting moved around the country and as technology and consumer demands evolved. At times, these market forces led to consolidation of capacity. Structural change is generally thought to result in economic gains over the long run, but possible negative consequences can include local job losses, economic instability, shifts in capital flows, or declines in local market demands for resources. Globalization can accelerate or alter the nature of structural change.

Globalization, consolidation, and structural change during the past decade contributed to a recent downturn in domestic consumption of certain forest products and corresponding loss of industrial capacity and related jobs, increased imports, decreased exports, and lower stumpage prices. Globalization and structural change contributed to the following:

Domestic consumption of paper and paperboard declined by 7% from a peak of 103 million tons in 1999 to 96 million tons in 2003, and then increased by 4% in 2004. By 2006, consumption still remained below the 1999 peak level.

According to the Forest Resources Association (2003), by 2002 annual volumes of pulpwood receipts at U.S. pulp mills had declined by 16% since peaking in 1994, although volume rose by 4% from 2002 to 2004.

Domestic hardwood lumber consumption in furniture declined from 3.3 billion board feet in 2000 to about 1.7 billion board feet in 2003; for pallets, the decline was from about 5 billion board feet to 3 billion board feet.

Economic globalization contributed to significant abatement of growth in U.S. timber harvest because some processing capacity was lost to competitors in other countries.

About one out of six U.S. paper and paperboard mills have closed since the mid-1990s.

One out of every three jobs at U.S. pulp and paper mills have been eliminated since the early 1990s because of consolidation, cost-cutting, and productivity improvements.

Nearly 40 North Carolina furniture plants have closed since 2001.

The number of major softwood sawmills in the United States declined from 850 in 1995 to 700 in 2004, with a 37% increase in average capacity as older mills were replaced with larger ones.

In a decade, the percentage of U.S. sales of wood household furniture imports, primarily from China, increased from 20% to more than 50% and continues to expand.

Since 1990, imports of softwood lumber increased from 27.1% (12.1 billion board feet) of consumption to 38% (25 billion board feet).

Imports of oriented strandboard (OSB) increased from 1.3 billion ft^2 (19% of consumption) in 1990 to 8.5 billion ft^2 (39% of consumption) in 2002.

Southern Pine pulpwood stumpage prices peaked about 1997, declined to half that level by 2002, and have not recovered to previous peak levels.

Globalization and structural change have contributed to declines in exports of timber products from the United States. New suppliers have emerged in world markets, and the nature of demand has changed for some countries. For example, softwood log export volume from the four West Coast states declined from 3.7 billion board feet in 1990 to less than one billion board feet in 2003. Much of the decline was due to reduced shipments to China, Japan, and South Korea. Exports of softwood lumber, plywood, and wood chips from the United States have also declined.

Structural change and economic globalization have many implications for evaluation of the status and trends of renewable resources. For example, imports of timber products decrease domestic harvest and thereby affect commonly used measures of resource condition such as the growth removal ratio for roundwood. Structural change and globalization should also be key considerations in evaluation of future returns from forest management because they affect stumpage prices and costs of forest management.

Implications of economic globalization and structural change summarized in the Interim Update of the RPA Assessment (USDA Forest Service 2007) included the following. Expansion of free trade policies has affected U.S. competitiveness in forest products and mineral and energy resources, and accelerated restructuring and consolidation of the U.S. forest products industries. The United States is expected to continue to be a net importer of timber products, as well as numerous mineral and energy products. High levels of goods imports and continued high rates of paper recycling resulted in U.S. timber harvest increasing at a slower rate than in the last half of the 20th century. Imports and loss of domestic processing capacity reduce domestic timber harvest, which affects the age–class distribution of domestic forests, which in turn affects habitat for plants and animals, biodiversity, and other measures of forest resource condition. A slowing in the growth of stumpage prices caused by imports reduces expectations for long-term returns for forest management, raising questions about incentives for sustainable forest management. Globalization has been associated with the loss of domestic capacity in forest industry and several mineral industries. The historic comparative advantage of some U.S. industries is now challenged by rising imports and structural changes in manufacturing. Related effects are loss of jobs and income, which is particularly problematic for natural-resource-dependent communities with few other economic development options.

Preface

This report was initially drafted in summer 2004 as a technical document supporting the Interim Update of the RPA Assessment (USDA Forest Service 2007). It was circulated widely for review, and some of its key findings are incorporated into the Interim RPA Assessment Update. This report contains many charts and makes reference to a wide variety of data trends across the U.S. forest sector. Most of the charts and data, although not all, were updated since 2004, but general findings and observations that were made in 2004 have remained valid since then (at least to 2006). In the RPA context, some of the effects of economic globalization and effects of the recent downturn in U.S. industrial production (2000 to 2002) were recognized and incorporated into the RPA resource outlook as early as the 2001 RPA timber assessment (particularly effects on the pulp and paper sector).

From the vantage point of 2006, overall U.S. industrial production has largely recovered from the downturn in the early part of the decade, with positive implications for growth in sectors such as pulp and paper. The recovery from the downturn was actually anticipated and projected in the 2001 RPA timber assessment, but (as projected) the growth rates in industries such as pulp and paper remain much lower than in the decades prior to the recent downturn, as does the projected growth rate for overall U.S. timber harvest. The housing sector along with lumber and wood panel demands experienced a continued boom through 2005, which only began to wane in 2006, but imports of lumber and wood panels remained at historically high levels while exports have declined.

From a positive perspective, the U.S. forest sector remains a large and important economic sector in the United States, but this report serves as a reminder that future growth cannot be taken for granted and will depend on a spirit that is competitive, innovative, and forward-looking, as it has always in the past. However, as recognized in this report and related RPA studies, the future of the U.S. forest product industry and similarly the future of forestry and forest management in the United States are increasingly dependent on sustaining the global competitiveness of the U.S. forest sector.

The purpose of this report is to review important structural changes that have occurred in the U.S. forest sector under the influence of economic globalization for about the past decade and to interpret some of the implications of globalization and structural change in terms of sustaining forestry and forest management activities in the United States. This report is not intended to review effects of economic globalization around the world or to compare effects of globalization in other economic sectors but is focused instead on effects and changes that can be observed specifically in the U.S. forest sector in recent years. The report fulfills its purpose by providing discussion of a series of interrelated topics as listed in the contents.

Globalization and Structural Change in the U.S. Forest Sector

An Evolving Context for Sustainable Forest Management

Peter Ince, Research Forester
Forest Products Laboratory, Madison, Wisconsin

Albert Schuler, Research Economist
Northern Research Station, Princeton, West Virginia

Henry Spelter, Economist
Forest Products Laboratory, Madison, Wisconsin

William Luppold, Economist
Northern Research Station, Princeton, West Virginia

Introduction

Economic Globalization

Globalization refers to the ongoing expansion of global interconnectedness in society and culture (Held and others 1999), and economic globalization refers to expansion of global interconnectedness in commerce, business, and capital investments. Economic globalization was advanced in recent years by free trade policies and rules of commerce that helped expand global trade and global competition. One key hypothesis is that economic globalization accelerated business responses to competition. As markets were exposed to more global competition, businesses were compelled to become more efficient and cost-competitive than they might be in a strictly local or regional context. The following observations appear, for example, in a recent U.S. Department of Commerce report on manufacturing in America:

> Barriers to trade have fallen rapidly over the past decade. Innovations in communications, computing, and distribution have accelerated the design, production, and delivery of goods. Improved production processes have spread rapidly throughout the world. Private investment now flows largely unimpeded across national borders as investors seek the highest rates of return. All these factors equate to unprecedented global competition for capital and markets. Because manufactured goods make up the bulk of international trade, the competition is especially strong. Taken together, the effects of technology and globalization accelerate the competitive pressures to lower costs and increase productivity (U.S. Department of Commerce 2004).

Globalization and free trade have also a strong economic rationale, apart from any other benefits or consequences, as they tend to yield economic prosperity worldwide. Former U.S. Treasury Secretary John Snow made the following statement recently:

> The world economy is more connected than ever before, as a result of the dramatic expansion of trade and capital flows in recent decades. Financial markets are now closely integrated and businesses increasingly serve customers across the world . . . On the matter of the importance of trade, here are some cold hard facts: trade benefits both emerging and industrial nations, trade leads to increased global prosperity, trade raises global standards of living, and trade creates jobs.[1]

The competitive response of businesses to economic globalization exemplifies free enterprise, the continuous process of economic optimization through reallocation of capital. Many years ago the noted economist Joseph Schumpeter described this general process as "creative destruction"—the continuous liquidation and reinvestment of capital into more efficient and profitable enterprises using newer technology or more modern equipment or shifting production from one region to another. Newer technology and more efficient production capacity will typically push out the older and less efficient. Ever since the dawn of the modern industrial era, capital stock has continuously undergone renewal through investment of cash flow from existing enterprises into larger or more efficient production facilities, or from one region to another depending on comparative advantage. For example, the U.S. textile industry witnessed the first large-scale factory development in New England in the early 19th century (Tucker 1984), but later shifted to the South in pursuit of cheaper labor, and then eventually lost ground in more recent years to firms in Asia and Latin America. Likewise, forest product industry capacity growth shifted from the Pacific Northwest to the South in the 1980s and 1990s, associated with reduced access to timber supply from public forestlands in the Northwest, with more readily available timber resources and newer production facilities in the South.

As import competition intensified since the early 1990s, major U.S. industrial sectors such as textiles and forest products experienced a wave of reduced profits, declining capacity growth, and business consolidation. Competition

---

[1]Prepared remarks by U.S. Treasury Secretary John Snow; delivered to the U.S. Chamber of Commerce; Wednesday, January 7, 2004.

and reduced profitability compelled U.S. manufacturers to consolidate, to more rapidly reduce labor inputs and production costs, to outsource supplies of materials or goods to other countries, or move production capacity abroad. Wood household furniture production, for example, declined in the United States, as it was offset by a surge in wood furniture imports. Throughout, manufacturing costs commonly were reduced through consolidation or adoption of technologies that provided increased automation and efficiency, such as computerized controls in manufacturing. Many older or less efficient pulp and paper mills were closed in recent years. Efficiency gains, shifts in capacity, and other technological changes deeply affected employment, capacity growth, resource use, and local opportunities for sustainable resource development. Meanwhile, a U.S. housing boom was stimulated in recent years by cheap financing, made available in large part by record trade deficits and expanded foreign purchases of U.S. financial assets. Recent surges in demand for softwood lumber and structural wood panels in housing construction with limited capacity expansion contributed to strong cyclical inflation in lumber and wood panel prices and rising imports. Shifts in foreign investment, higher interest rates, and limited growth in payroll employment might contribute to an eventual decline in housing construction, among other potential future legacies of economic globalization.

Structural Change

Largely irreversible changes in economic relationships can arise from the process of "creative destruction," the competitive replacement of older and less efficient means of production by more efficient means of production. As more efficient technologies are adopted, more efficient business relationships are established, or more cost-efficient production facilities are built, the changes become largely irreversible because it stands against the logic of economic behavior to abandon efficiency gains or cost savings. Such change in an economy is called structural change (as opposed to more transitory cyclical change). Structural change can have lasting social, economic, or environmental consequences. Structural change or "creative destruction" is generally thought to result in economic gain over the long run, but other negative consequences can stem from structural change, at least in the short run, including local job losses, economic instability, shifts in capital flows, or declines in local market demands for resources.

The initial hypothesis in this report is that structural change was accelerated by economic globalization since the early 1990s, as import competition compelled U.S. manufacturers to pursue more rapid cost reduction through consolidation, productivity gains, reshaping of production capacity, and outsourcing of labor or material supply, with related shifts in historical patterns of resource demands. The genesis of recent trends in globalization and structural change in manufacturing is highlighted in the following excerpt:

Over the past two decades, three separate, powerful trends have reshaped the manufacturing sector globally. The first is the revolution in technology that has been under way for two decades, raising productivity in manufacturing and reducing costs worldwide. The second is the significant reduction in barriers to trade, particularly with respect to trade in manufactured goods. The third is the end to political divisions that have segmented markets for more than 70 years and the corresponding emergence of Russia, China, and other countries in the world trading system . . . The practical effect on U.S. manufacturers of the three trends described above has been to increase the availability of new sources of low-cost labor and manufacturing capacity. Indeed, the trends have not only made it available, they have also made it an important competitive issue. In a global economy in which both goods and capital are mobile, but labor is not, manufacturers' tapping of lower cost labor by importing it in the form of lower cost parts, components, and—increasingly—finished goods is simply a function of trying to stay competitive in a global economy. Hence, the trend toward sourcing parts and components globally is driven by powerful competitive forces and is here to stay. Manufacturers now have the ability to manage global supply chains effectively, which allows them to source from the lowest cost supplier globally and, as a competitive matter, forces hem to do so in order to remain competitive themselves (U.S. Department of Commerce 2004).

Job losses and job instability are among obvious social consequences of structural change in manufacturing. Federal Reserve Chairman Alan Greenspan recognized, for example, that elevated rates of return offered by newer technologies during the 1990s were largely because of reduced labor inputs and costs per unit of output.[2] Investment returns for the same technologies were lower in Europe and Japan because businesses there faced higher costs of displacing workers than in the United States, where displacement was more readily countenanced both by law and by culture. Because costs of dismissing workers were lower, costs of hiring and risks associated with expanding employment were also lower. Thus, a benefit of "creative destruction" with fluid labor and rehiring practices was lower structural unemployment in the United States, compared to Europe, for example (U.S. Department of Commerce 2004). However, there was also a secular (long-run) displacement of labor in U.S. manufacturing relative to U.S. industrial output (reflecting secular productivity gains in manufacturing). Displacement of workers in manufacturing was an ongoing structural change reflecting technological progress and automation over decades, but that change became accelerated since the early 1990s as industry responded to import competition

---

[2]Alan Greenspan, *Structural change in the new economy*, presentation by Federal Reserve Chairman before National Governors' Association, 92nd Annual Meeting, State College, Pennsylvania, July 11, 2000.

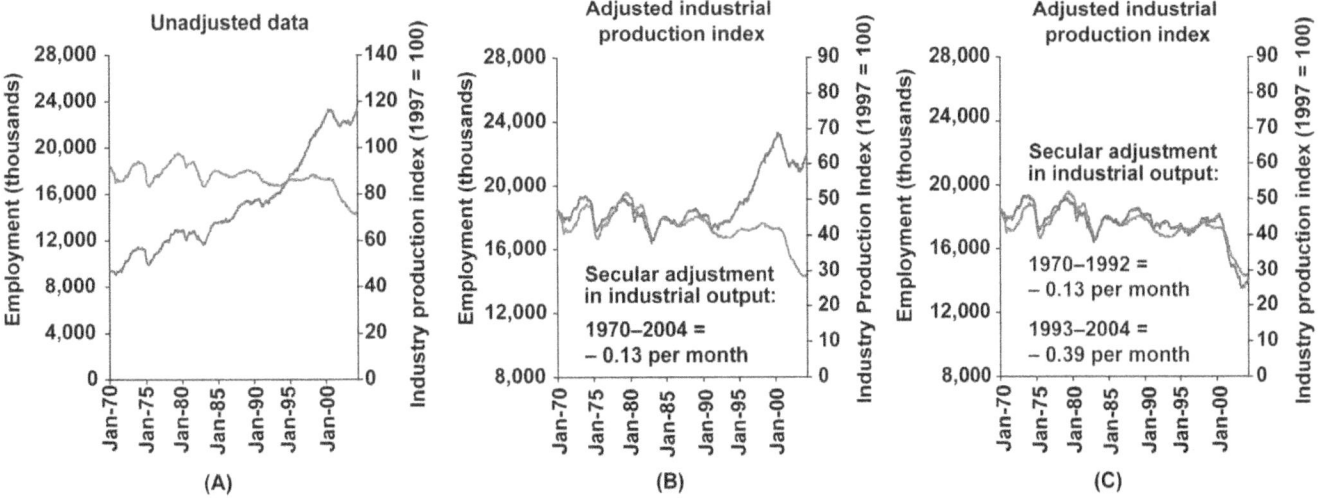

Figure 1—U.S. manufacturing employment (green line, BLS 2006a, b) and index of industrial production (blue line, Federal Reserve (2006b)), 1970–2004 (A), and the same data with secular adjustment of industrial production at – 0.13 index value per month for entire period (B), and – 0.13 per month from 1970 to 1992, and – 0.39 per month from 1993 to 2004 (C).

primarily by downsizing labor inputs with rapid productivity gains and outsourcing.

Historical data on U.S. industrial production and manufacturing employment show that ongoing structural change became significantly accelerated since the early 1990s, when economic globalization began to exert a much stronger influence on the U.S. economy. Since 1991, U.S. goods imports tripled and the U.S. trade deficit in goods expanded 10-fold, and shortly after 1991 the ongoing rate of labor displacement (or productivity gain) in U.S. manufacturing began to accelerate rapidly. As shown in Figure 1(A), the raw index of U.S. industrial production generally increased since 1970, while employment in U.S. manufacturing generally declined with ongoing or secular productivity gains. In addition, as shown in Figure 1(B), a secular adjustment in the industrial production index of – 0.13 every month can account for all divergence between the output index and employment trend from 1970 to around 1992, but after 1992 the two trends still diverge despite the constant adjustment. As shown in Figure 1(C), the secular adjustment required to merge the two trends from 1993 to 2004 is – 0.39 per month, which is three times the secular adjustment needed to merge the trends up to 1992. Thus, data show clearly that a significant shift occurred in the secular rate of labor displacement in U.S. manufacturing during the period when the U.S. trade deficit in goods experienced a record 10-fold expansion and U.S. imports of goods more than tripled since 1991. The shift in the ongoing rate of labor displacement shows that structural change in manufacturing became accelerated as the United States gained much wider exposure to import competition since the early 1990s. Downsizing of labor input was facilitated by ongoing technological trends in manufacturing, with computerization favoring increased automation. This shift in manufacturing employment was

reflected in recent years by much slower growth in nationwide payroll employment and real employee compensation.

In recent years, economic globalization also accelerated another aspect of structural change or "creative destruction"—outsourcing of manufacturing from the United States to other countries where lower wages, less stringent safety or health regulations, different tax structures, or low real dollar exchange rates afforded real production cost advantages. Around 3 million U.S. manufacturing jobs were lost from 2000 to 2004, attributable in large part to productivity gains compelled by increased global competition, and several hundred thousand of those jobs were lost reportedly because of direct outsourcing of production, mainly to low-income countries (Nussbaum 2004). Thus, beyond pressures in education and training to prepare and adapt fewer U.S. workers to effectively run new technologies and achieve higher productivity, economic globalization added new pressures on businesses and workers to compete with global enterprises expanding in other countries that have lower wages and lower standards of living.

As growth in industrial output subsided in the United States in recent years, it led to declining capital investment and engineering activity, while capital investment and capacity growth expanded overseas in countries like China. Some firms also began to outsource technical support and service jobs to skilled workers in low-income countries. Furthermore, the skills and technological infrastructure of manufacturing have begun to move abroad along with manufacturing capacity and jobs, leaving a legacy of limited capacity growth in the United States. With limited U.S. capacity growth, any rapid upturn in demand for U.S. industrial output might be expected to ignite inflationary tendencies, particularly if the exchange value of the dollar continued decreasing as it did from 2002 to 2004, but long-run inflation is held in check by imports of low-cost foreign goods.

Beyond the consequences for employment and development, globalization and structural change left also a legacy of structural shifts in raw material use in certain sectors, such as the forest sector. The shift of manufacturing overseas, for example, led to a decline in U.S. demand for paperboard in packaging (such as corrugated boxes), contributing to structural shifts in demand for pulpwood and other fiber inputs. Likewise, shifts in advertising toward global electronic media (compared with local print media) contributed to structural change in paper demand, with declining U.S. newsprint demand and declining print advertising expenditures. Declining U.S. wood furniture production with increased imports and outsourcing of furniture production to low-income countries resulted in shifts in local demands for hardwood timber and veneer. In general, globalization and structural change introduced new pressures and uncertainties in the forest sector, a sector previously accustomed to growth in demand but recently facing declining domestic demands and a more limited economic contribution to U.S. gross domestic product (GDP).

Escalation in the exchange value of the U.S. dollar from 1996 to 2002 (with declining real dollar exchange rates) also contributed to record goods trade deficits. The stronger dollar attracted imports of goods while making U.S. manufactured goods more expensive and therefore less competitive abroad. Since 2002, the real exchange value of the dollar receded, a trend that restored some competitiveness for U.S. manufacturers and was leading toward recovery for pulp and paper demand. However, reduced output capacity and closures of many pulp and paper mills in recent years are structural changes that imply gradual recovery and also create a near-term inflationary potential for pulp and paper commodities. Thus, the legacy of globalization is likely to remain significant, even though import competition may temporarily recede with currency fluctuations.

Economic globalization and structural change imply a need for investment in human capital and technology, focusing on globally competitive enterprises. However, the numbers of U.S. workers employed in manufacturing have dwindled in recent years, with prodigious gains in labor productivity. Productivity gains and outsourcing led to an 18% drop in overall U.S. manufacturing employment in the period from 1997 to 2003. Manufacturing employment reached 17.3 million in 1997 and remained near that level up to the year 2000; however, it declined by several million, falling to 14.3 million by the end of 2003 (BLS 2004). At the same time, new U.S. immigrants accounted for over half of the growth in the U.S. labor force from 2000 to 2003, and new immigrants gained more than 300,000 jobs in U.S. manufacturing during that period (Sum and others 2003). Furthermore, research shows that import competition from low-income countries favors more capital-intensive U.S. business enterprises versus labor-intensive enterprises (Bernard and others 2002).

Increased global cost competition, particularly in mass commodity markets (such as steel, textiles, and also forest product commodities) has led to increased interest in specialized niche markets or customized products that may provide better revenue or some relief from the volatility and cost/price competition that is characteristic of commodity markets. The interest in niche markets might suggest that smaller scale enterprises could prosper in the context of economic globalization, but there is little evidence for this notion. Instead, the development of niche markets or specialized products has been accompanied by a continuation of trends toward larger scale and more globally oriented enterprises, which are generally seeking to gain market advantages via product branding, product identity, or product value in increasingly competitive global markets.

Although there are certainly exceptions, recent trends in the U.S. forest product industry indicate likewise that generally larger and more capital-intensive enterprises are more likely to survive global competition than smaller less capital-intensive or more labor-intensive enterprises. Meanwhile, competing countries are focusing public resources on global opportunities, with the Canadian government, for example, providing $7 million Canadian dollars in 2004 for the "Canada Wood" program to develop markets for Canadian export wood products (U.S. Department of Commerce 2004).

Globalization and the U.S. Forest Sector

A Brief Overview

Economic globalization has been an important contributor to structural change in recent years. It has had a growing influence on the overall U.S. economy since the early 1990s, and a growing influence on the U.S. forest sector as well. With liberalized trade policies and a strong U.S. economy in the 1990s, the real exchange value of the U.S. dollar soared above its historical average from 1997 through 2004. With its strong dollar, the United States was a global engine of economic growth, tripling the value of goods imports (from 0.49 trillion dollars in 1991 to 1.47 trillion dollars by 2004). This resulted in the largest goods trade deficits of any country in history (783 billion dollars by 2005, a 10-fold expansion since 1991) (BEA 2006). The flood of competitive and often less expensive foreign goods reduced output and profits for U.S. manufacturers, resulting in consolidation, downsizing, and other structural changes (changes reflected also in the U.S. forest sector).

Overall U.S. industrial production (measured by the Federal Reserve index) began to weaken during the Asian financial crisis of 1997, then peaked in the year 2000 and dropped precipitously in 2001, along with rollbacks in capital investment expenditures and business growth. The 2001 recession (measured by consecutive quarterly declines in U.S. GDP in that year) was thus largely a business-led recession, reflecting primarily declining profitability and growth in U.S.

manufacturing and business in general. Economic stimuli of lower interest rates and tax reductions helped restore economic growth and contributed to a housing boom from 2002 to 2005, but U.S. industrial output only began to show a sustained trend toward recovery late in 2003 and 2004.

The forest sector broadly subtends a spectrum of enterprises and activities ranging from forestry and forest management to forest product industries and other forest-dependent business enterprises, including recreational enterprises, non-wood products, and a range of other ecosystem services. In the United States, the forest sector encompasses both public and privately owned forestlands, from which wood raw materials are harvested to produce forest products. This report focuses on primary forest product industries, such as pulp, paper, and paperboard, and the so-called solid-wood industries, including lumber, particleboard, plywood, and other wood products. A number of large secondary industries or other economic sectors depend heavily on primary forest products, such as the shipping and warehousing sector—dependent on corrugated boxes, shipping containers, and wooden pallets; the publication and print advertising sector—dependent on newsprint and printing paper; the housing and construction sector—dependent on soft- and hardwood lumber, particleboard, and plywood; and the furniture sector—dependent on hardwood lumber, veneer, and particleboard. In general, economic globalization affected all of these industries in recent years, and thus in turn economic globalization has affected the broader forest sector in general.

The U.S. pulp and paper industry, for example, was deeply affected by economic globalization and structural changes since the mid-1990s. Domestic purchases of paper and paperboard generally declined since 1999, from a peak of 103 million tons to 96 million tons in 2003, as expansion of goods imports led to decline in overall manufacturing and corresponding declines in domestic demands for paper and paperboard in packaging and print advertising (AF&PA 2003). Commodity products account for the bulk of product volume in the pulp and paper sector, such as newsprint, market pulp, linerboard, or corrugating medium used for corrugated boxes or other standard grades of paper or paperboard. Commodity products can be readily substituted in many cases by imports. Thus, when the U.S. dollar gained in value from 1996 to 2002, cost competitiveness of U.S. producers waned, and U.S. exports of pulp, paper, and paperboard subsided; imports increased, and the trade deficit for pulp, paper, and paperboard products widened from 1 million tons to 9 million tons (AF&PA 2003). More significantly, reduced demand, increased imports, and excess production capacity since the mid-1990s contributed to a downward spiral in U.S. pulp and paper revenues and profits, with a decline in net sales from $184 billion in 2000 to $145 billion in 2003 (U.S. Department of Commerce 2004). Weak profits led to consolidation and permanent closure

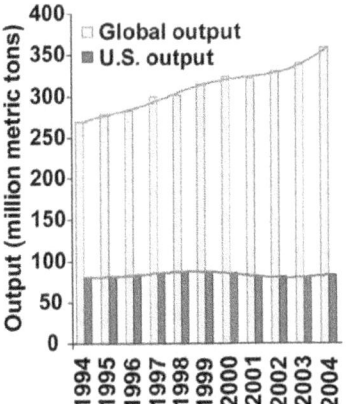

Figure 2—Annual paper and paperboard production, 1994 to 2004, showing total global output and U.S. output alone (Paperloop 2004). Globally, paper and paperboard output was up by 91 million metric tons (+ 34%) from 1994 to 2004, but there was little net increase in U.S. output over that decade. Essentially, global consumers went outside the United States to meet growing demands of lower cost competitors in Asia, Latin America, and Europe.

of many U.S. pulp and paper mills, approximately one out of every six mills since the mid-1990s (many with smaller than average capacity). Declining industry employment witnessed the elimination of approximately one out of every three jobs at U.S. pulp and paper mills since the mid-1990s.

From a U.S. perspective, it might appear that pulp and paper is a mature or perhaps declining sector, but the pulp and paper sector is a growth industry globally. One of the lessons of economic globalization is that structural change has disparate effects on different regions. This fact is illustrated well in Figure 2, which shows annual global paper and paperboard production, along with annual production for the United States alone from 1994 to 2004. Whereas annual U.S. paper and paperboard production leveled out and declined for a period during that decade, annual paper and paperboard production rose by 91 million metric tons globally (+ 34%). Just the increase in global output during that decade exceeded current annual U.S. production.

Furthermore, after steady growth in U.S. wood pulp production through the 20th century, the decline in U.S. wood pulp production that occurred since the mid-1990s came as an abrupt shock. Annual U.S. consumption of pulpwood at wood pulp mills had dropped by about 15% by 2003, off by 40 million green tons since peaking in 1994 (FRA 2003). Globalization and consolidation in pulp, paper, and overall manufacturing thus deeply affected pulpwood markets as well as economic growth and development in the pulp and paper sector (these trends are discussed in more detail in subsequent sections).

Although smaller in scale than pulp and paper, the U.S. wood furniture sector experienced proportionately greater inroads through globalization and consolidation since the early 1990s. A decade ago, imports accounted for just 20% of product value sold in the U.S. household wood furniture market, but imports have soared to more than 50% of the market value and continue to expand. The largest share of expansion in wood furniture imports is from China, now the leading source of U.S. wood furniture imports, and also a major source of wood furniture components. Expansion of wood furniture and component imports from China over the past decade is a classical story of competitive displacement of U.S. manufacturing capacity and employment by much cheaper overseas labor (the story is discussed in greater detail in subsequent sections of this report). In brief, wood furniture production and wood furniture component manufacture are fairly labor intensive, and typically wage rates in Chinese furniture factories are less than 10% of those in the United States. Thus, it is more profitable in many cases to import raw wood into China, produce furniture or furniture components there, and ship the product to market in the United States (or elsewhere) than to produce it in the United States. Moreover, entrepreneurs from China, the United States, and elsewhere have facilitated expansion of production capacity in China, while rapidly developing expertise and technology to produce quality furniture products in China. Consequently, domestic use of hardwood lumber in furniture production in the United States has declined in recent years, particularly higher quality hardwood lumber.

In both the pulp and paper and furniture sectors, economic globalization and import competition led to structural changes. The sifting and winnowing of production capacity with closure of less competitive facilities has led to the survival of firms and plant facilities likely to be more efficient and competitive, with lower average labor input requirements and more productive processes. In the furniture sector, some firms have gained market share and expanded by adopting the strategy of importing wood furniture parts for final product assembly in the United States, while also adopting more laborsaving technological improvements. Logically, the surviving industry may thus be better suited than before to meet global competition, and if the dollar continues to weaken, as it has since 2002, the U.S. industry will be better positioned to take advantage of global markets. However, other complexities cloud that outlook; capital investment in the U.S. pulp and paper industry has subsided over the past decade, whereas overseas capacity expansion in new and more efficient production facilities has continued (in Europe and China, for example). In many cases, foreign producers retain competitive cost advantages relative to U.S. producers, although costs vary among mills and are influenced by currency exchange rates. In

the furniture sector, U.S. producers still retain some leads in automation and productivity, but it becomes increasingly difficult to compete as U.S. wages generally increase from year to year while overseas technology continues to be modernized and average wages in places like China remain very low. Generally, lower wages abroad also provide much lower capital investment costs (because of lower plant construction costs with cheaper labor).

For those forest product industries such as softwood lumber that serve primarily the housing sector, along with particleboard and plywood, the relatively robust housing boom of recent years afforded some shelter from economic globalization and the recent flood of goods imports. With no significant international trade in housing construction or remodeling services, the U.S. housing sector itself is somewhat insulated from direct global competition. However, even in the housing sector, globalization and consolidation have begun to have some effects. One example is development and expansion of steel-frame housing, which substitutes for wood-frame housing (and partially eliminates the need for softwood lumber framing material). The steel industry has been subject to intense competition from imported steel products, particularly in commodity steel products produced and sold on the global market. The U.S. steel industry has sought new avenues for product development over the past decade, particularly expansion of domestic markets for fabricated steel products that might be less exposed to trade competition. This launched an array of new steel framing products and market initiatives that have begun to have some effect on material use in housing construction.

In addition, although domestic housing demands are still the largest market for U.S. "solid wood" products, significant inroads were made by imported wood products in U.S. markets since the early 1990s, while export markets were increasingly flooded by products from foreign competitors. Imports thus accounted for much of the growth in U.S. softwood lumber and structural panel consumption. For example, in 1990 U.S. softwood lumber imports were 27.1% of consumption or 12.1 billion board feet, almost entirely from Canada, while U.S. consumption of softwood lumber was 44.7 billion board feet. By 2002, softwood lumber imports were 21.0 billion board feet, 37.4% of total consumption (56.1 billion board feet), while 19.1 billion board feet was from Canada (34.0% of consumption). For the dominant structural panel product used in housing, oriented strandboard (OSB), trends were much the same. In 1990, the United States imported 1.31 billion ft² representing 18.9% of U.S. consumption, 6.95 billion ft². In 2002, imports of OSB were 8.47 billion ft² representing 38.7% of U.S. consumption. Softwood plywood imports also increased, despite declining demand. In 1990, the United States was essentially self-reliant in plywood, importing a mere 0.2% of consumption from abroad, with consumption at 20.7 billion ft². By 2002, the United States was dependent on imports for 0.91 billion ft², 5.8% of total consumption, 15.7 billion ft². Thus, shifts in trade resulted in substitution of imports for domestic production, while at the same time there was a notable loss of growth in exports; for both lumber and wood panels, generally contributing to structural shifts in consumption of wood raw material in the United States.

Structural changes that unfolded in the era of rapid globalization and consolidation since the early 1990s changed also the outlook for U.S. timber demand. The recent 2001 RPA timber assessment recognized, for example, that U.S. pulpwood demand peaked in the mid-1990s. Gradual recovery in pulpwood demand was projected in the decades ahead, and thus annual U.S. timber harvest was projected to increase gradually from around 17 billion ft³ currently to 22 billion ft³ by 2040 (Haynes 2003). However, before the 1990s, pulpwood demand was increasing more rapidly, and thus it was reasonable then to project that overall U.S. timber harvest could reach 27 billion ft³ in 2040, as projected in the 1989 RPA timber assessment (Haynes 1990). The 5 billion ft³ adjustment in projected U.S. annual timber harvest is mainly attributable to the recent downturn in pulpwood demand (a consequence of industry globalization and consolidation, as well as increased paper recycling). Other adjustments were also relevant, such as reduced growth in fuelwood demand and reduced log and chip exports. The nationwide timber demand outlook clearly changed, and is now much lower than previously projected, largely because of the effects of globalization, consolidation, and structural change.

The reduction in projected timber demand also changed the outlook for forest resource conditions nationwide. For example, the 1989 RPA timber assessment (RPA 1989) had projected that U.S. timber growing stock volume would no longer increase because expanding harvests would match forest growth in the years ahead. By contrast, the recent 2001 RPA timber assessment (RPA 2001) projected a 40% increase in timber growing stock volume over the next 50 years, which happens to match the percentage increase of the past 50 years. Hardwood harvest was still projected to increase (about one-third by 2050). However, softwood harvest on non-plantation forestland was projected to decline by about 25%, as harvest on softwood plantations (chiefly Southern Pine plantations) was projected to expand to almost 55% of softwood timber supply by 2050. Thus, according to recent U.S. timber assessments, the outlook for decades ahead (over the next 50 years) is for very little increase in total timber harvest nationwide on the roughly 450 million acres (over 90%) of commercially available U.S. timberland that is projected to remain in natural forest cover (apart from managed plantations), with hardwood harvest increasing and softwood harvest decreasing on those lands. Tens of millions of acres of additional forestland will also remain preserved in parks, wilderness, and other reserves. Forest age structure will thus become increasingly mature, particularly for softwood timber in the U.S. West, where

public forestlands predominate. Forest management will increasingly face conditions of accumulating timber inventories and limited growth in demand. These conditions include accumulating volumes of timber in need of thinning to reduce fire hazard but limited growth in markets for timber. In addition, future markets will likely afford less robust growth in forestry revenues and thus a more limited contribution of forestry to overall GDP growth. The forest sector contribution to U.S. GDP has in fact declined since the mid-1990s (U.S. Department of Commerce 2002). Future policies and programs related to forestry and sustainable forest management thus need to be shaped in an evolving context of economic globalization and structural change, a topic discussed further in this report.

Relevance to Sustaining Forest Management

The evolving trends of economic globalization and structural change occur in the broader context of human development. Globalization exerts an influence on human development in economic, social, and environmental dimensions. Those three dimensions are also recognized internationally as core concerns of sustainable development (UN 2006). Hence, some scholars have questioned whether economic globalization and sustainable development are competing paradigms of human development, although throughout the world most governments generally support both free trade and sustainable development (Speth 2003).

Linking economic globalization to sustainable forest management is a complex issue, one discussed here only in the context of the U.S. forest sector. For example, over the past decade globalization and consolidation in forest products led to generally larger, more productive and cost-efficient U.S. mills on average, but fewer mills remain in operation. With growth in U.S. timber demand offset by imports, millions of acres of U.S. industrial forestland were sold in recent years by U.S. forest product firms to consolidate operations, reduce debt, or obtain favorable tax advantages (Fosgate 2002). Fourteen million acres of industrial timberland were sold nationwide in a recent 5-year period amid mergers and consolidations in the U.S. forest product industry according to research at Warnell School of Forest Resources, University of Georgia (Fosgate 2002). Thus, globalization has reduced the direct role of large U.S. corporations in financing forest management in the United States. Economic benefits attributable to timber management are also less prominent (as reflected, for example, in the declining contribution of forestry to U.S. GDP since the mid-1990s). Globalization has thus shifted the outlook for forestry and forest management options, and may have altered the political and economic base of support for sustainable forest management in the United States (at least in the private sector).

According to economic theory, globalization and free trade should enhance economic prosperity on a global scale, as capital moves more freely to the most productive uses and locations. Thus, free trade enhances creation of wealth or private capital, but the form or allocation of capital is usually not constrained by trade policy. Free trade policy generally avoids intrinsic constraints on the form of capital or how accumulated private capital is to be managed, and indeed placing constraints on the investment or liquidation of capital is generally antithetical to capitalist free enterprise. Thus, although globalization and free trade offer benefits of increased global prosperity, it does not immediately follow that global prosperity will contribute positively to sustainable forest management in the United States or toward purposes such as monitoring and protection of biological diversity in forest ecosystems. Nor does it necessarily follow that global prosperity will—in the longer run—support sustainable forest management in the United States. The policy of free trade supports global free enterprise and capitalism, and it may or may not support activities such as environmental protection or ecosystem management. Logically, the policy of free trade will support those activities only if they are positively connected to global enterprise development or capitalism.

Thus, a direct policy course toward sustaining capital investment in the U.S. forest sector would be to focus public programs and infrastructure on helping to sustain the global competitiveness of the U.S. forest sector. To be effective, such programs and policies would need to discern which elements of the U.S. forest sector have a realistic potential for becoming more globally competitive and then support the most relevant research and development (R&D), education, and infrastructure development programs. A recently published national report on sustainable forest management notes the need to continue to provide the benefits that people derive from forest products, recreational and cultural experiences, ecosystem services, and community development. It states that economic development is a factor in maintaining the flow of these benefits (FS 2003). The report notes changes in levels of investment in forest management, industry, and R&D that would support continued economic development. The report does not —and was not intended to—suggest which types of R&D investments are most important to maintain the flow of values from forests. R&D investments may include those focused on forest product industry competitiveness or other forest-related enterprises such as ecotourism, or perhaps even enterprises that provide ecological services such as carbon sequestration.

If U.S. forest policy were to focus on sustaining competitiveness of U.S. forest product enterprises, it could entail efforts to develop more competitive technologies, but such technologies could also be adopted by global competitors. The cost-competitiveness of forest product technology generally increases with scale of production, increased automation, computerization, and capital intensity. As explained subsequently in this report, economic globalization and import competition have resulted in downsizing in employment and structural changes throughout the forest sector, but those changes have favored survival of larger scale and more capital-intensive forest product enterprises, while more labor-intensive or smaller scale and less capital-intensive enterprises have experienced proportionately greater decline.

Broad Perspectives on Economic Globalization

Expansion of the U.S. economy was associated in recent decades with increased trade and increased exposure to trade with countries that have much lower income per capita. Up to the mid-1970s, U.S. trade in goods was roughly balanced (with imports usually matched by exports), but since then the U.S. trade deficit greatly expanded, as producers in low-income countries gained much greater access to U.S. markets. In the period from the early 1970s to late 1990s, imports of goods from low-income countries were the fastest growing component of U.S. trade, increasing far more rapidly than total imports (Bernard and others 2002). Ubiquitous labels on many retail goods such as "Made in China" or "Made in Mexico" have displaced "Made in USA" or "Made in Japan." Imports increased far more rapidly than exports, and the U.S. trade balance in goods fell from a surplus of $8.9 billion in 1975 to a record goods trade deficit of –$783 billion in 2005, with a 10-fold increase in the deficit since 1991. From 1999 through 2005, the United States was importing an average of about $1.3 trillion of goods each year, more than double the annual level of goods imports a decade earlier, and goods imports reached $1.68 trillion in 2005.

Thus, in the span of just one generation, the United States went through a profound transition from a net goods exporter (as recently as 1975) to by far the world's largest net importer of goods, and compounding this shift was competition from low-income countries, which became a powerful force for reallocation of capital within and across U.S. industries. For example, in the period from the early 1970s to late 1990s, the reallocation of U.S. manufacturing involved shifting toward more capital- and skill-intensive industries in response to low-wage import competition. Research has shown that this was accomplished through the processes of plant closure (with more plant closures and less growth among less capital- and skill-intensive plants), by plant expansion (with higher growth among the more capital- or skill-intensive plants), and by product changes (with plants switching to products or sectors that were more capital- or skill-intensive than industries they left behind) (Bernard and others 2002). Plant closures, plant expansion, and changes in product mix are structural changes that resulted not only in shifts in employment opportunity but also in shifts of raw material demands.

In economics, production is understood to be the process by which inputs of labor, capital, energy, and raw materials are combined to produce output, and there is usually an ability to substitute one category of inputs for another. It would be expected therefore that the shift in manufacturing toward more capital- or skill-intensive enterprises would have effects on other inputs, such as offsetting inputs of labor or raw materials. These microeconomic effects were amplified by more profound economic developments that unfolded in the U.S. economy and in U.S. manufacturing since the mid-1990s. In particular, from 1996 to 2002 a surge in the real trade-weighted exchange value of the U.S. dollar contributed to rapid expansion of the U.S. trade deficit in goods, which led to an abrupt collapse of profits and growth in U.S. manufacturing during 2000 through 2001.

The Flood of Imports and Downturn in U.S. Industrial Production

In the 1990s, the United States emerged as the dominant global superpower and was the engine of global economic growth, but since the early 1990s the U.S. goods trade deficit also climbed to record levels. The United States supported free trade, but trade strongly favored imports of goods to the United States, particularly as the U.S. dollar increased in value. As shown in Figure 3, the U.S. trade deficit in goods generally followed gains in the broad nominal dollar value index (lagging by 2 to 3 years). As the U.S. dollar gained in value, foreign goods became relatively less expensive, favoring imports, while reducing domestic and export market competitiveness of U.S. manufacturers.

Since the early 1990s, U.S. goods imports and U.S. trade deficits rose to unprecedented levels. The U.S. goods trade deficit expanded by more than 10-fold in just 15 years, from $77 billion in 1991 to $783 billion in 2005 (Fig. 3). Overall goods imports more than tripled over the same period, reaching $1.68 trillion in 2004. The expansion of goods imports, particularly goods from low-income countries, had the effect of restraining price inflation, but weak pricing also reduced profitability for U.S. firms in sectors that were subject to import competition.

As goods imports soared, U.S. industrial output began to weaken in the late 1990s, and then declined, not recovering to 2000 peak levels until May 2004. Thus, U.S. industrial output diverged from capacity growth, leading to overcapacity, weak pricing, and a multiyear slowdown in industrial capacity growth, as illustrated in Figure 4.

The downturn in U.S. industrial production and rising tide of imported goods led to a decline in U.S. business investment due to overcapacity, market volatility, and reduced profitability in U.S. manufacturing. The manufacturing downturn starting in 2000 came on the heels of expanded capital investment in the late 1990s, and thus the downturn led to substantial overcapacity as shown by the divergence between Federal Reserve indexes of industrial production and production capacity (Fig. 4).

For firms in manufacturing, profits are usually very sensitive to the ratio of production volume to capacity, also known as capacity utilization. This is because capacity utilization

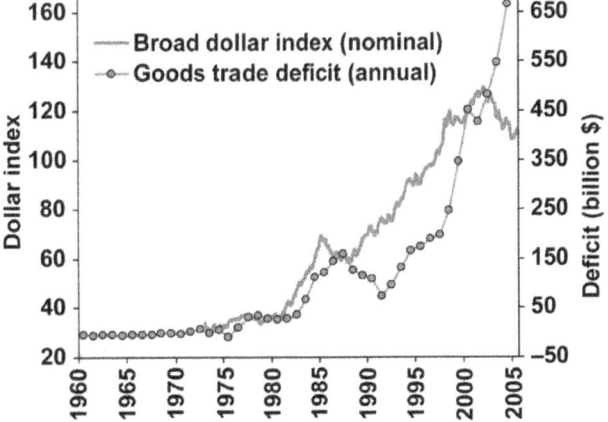

Figure 3—U.S. trade-weighted nominal broad dollar index (Federal Reserve 2006a) and annual U.S. trade deficit in goods (Census Bureau 2006a). Trade-weighted dollar index not available prior to 1973.

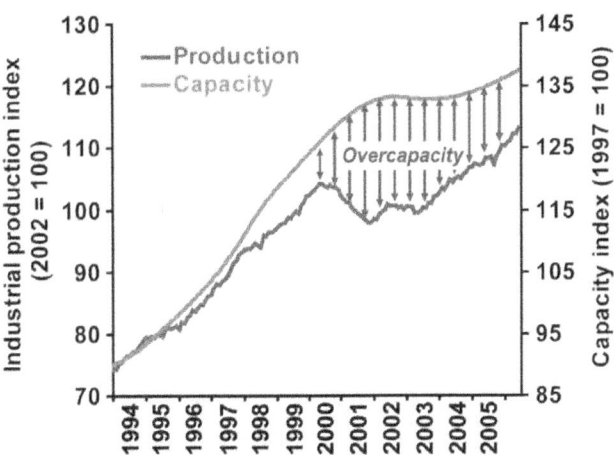

Figure 4—U.S. industrial production and production capacity indexes (Federal Reserve 2006a) showing divergence indicating overcapacity and slowdown in capacity growth.

is the principal determinant of short-run marginal supply in product markets, and thus it determines pricing leverage of manufacturing firms in those markets. When production falls substantially below existing production capacity, a condition of excess supply or overcapacity arises, so generally pricing leverage is weak and profits tend to decline. Expansion of overseas production capacity, economic globalization, and rising imports exacerbated conditions of excess capacity in the United States, and thus deflationary pressures were imported along with the flood of imported goods.

Overcapacity, declining output, rising goods imports, and weak prices led to a plunge in U.S. manufacturing profits and profitability in 2000 and 2001, illustrated in Figure 5 by quarterly after-tax profits and profits per dollar of sales for manufacturers. Thus, the downturn in U.S. industrial output spawned a rare business-led recession in 2001, with declining profits, weak investment, and little growth. An upturn

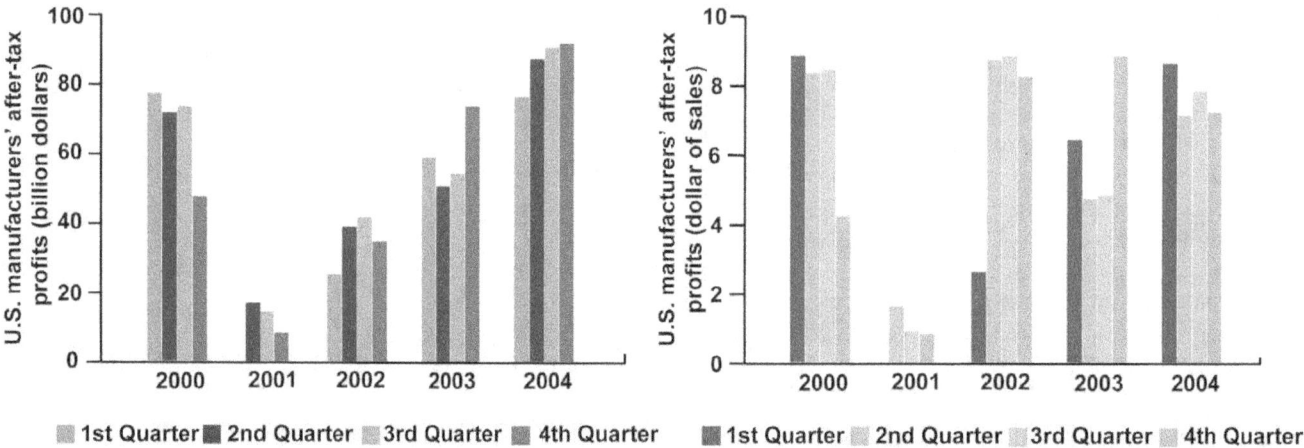

Figure 5—After-tax profits of U.S. manufacturers—billions of dollars per quarter, seasonally adjusted, and cents per dollar of sales quarterly, 2000 through 2004 (U.S. Department of Commerce 2005).

in profitability began in 2002, with nominal recovery in manufacturing profits by 2004, as downsizing of labor inputs, gains in productivity, outsourcing, and other cost-reducing efforts helped contribute to recovery in profits. However, a declining dollar depreciated somewhat the value of recent industry profits, and the downturn left a legacy of restructuring and realignment in U.S. manufacturing (Fig. 5).

Figure 6 illustrates recent year-over-year growth in U.S. industrial production (annual growth rate month to month), along with industrial capacity utilization as reported by the Federal Reserve (2006a). Following the downturn of U.S. industrial output in 2000 and 2001, growth was slow and uneven. By 2006, growth in U.S. industrial output had still not yet returned to peak growth rates of the late 1990s. Growth in industrial output faded during the 1997–1998 Asian Crisis (when export markets to Asia eroded with devaluation of some Asian currencies), and then growth collapsed in the broad manufacturing downturn and business recession of 2000 and 2001. Growth was barely positive in 2002, stalled in early 2003, and then growth resumed later in the year and into 2004, as the real exchange value of the dollar declined. Capacity utilization (which historically averaged around 82%) remained depressed at levels below 76% from 2001 through 2003, finally climbing above that level in early 2004. With exceptionally low capacity utilization in 2001–2003, pricing leverage for manufacturers remained weak. Manufactured commodity prices began to strengthen in late 2003 and 2004 as the dollar also weakened.

The downturn and gradual recovery of U.S. industrial output in recent years reflects broad structural change in the U.S. economy, particularly a decline in manufacturing relative to growth in the service sector, housing construction, and imports. Elements of structural change include the decline in manufacturing employment and a substantial shift in the rate of secular productivity gain (or labor displacement) in U.S.

manufacturing over the past decade (Fig. 1). Other elements of structural change include global shifts in production capacity and outsourcing, with growth of industrial production shifting to regions such as Asia, as well as corresponding structural shifts in global capacity growth and raw material use. One way to discuss implications of the structural change in U.S. manufacturing is to discuss the recent disconnect in data correlation between U.S. industrial production and U.S. GDP.

United States Industrial Output and Gross Domestic Product

Correlation between U.S. industrial output and GDP growth has important social and environmental relevance. For one thing, the national identity has long been connected to industrial accomplishments, and that identity has shaped how U.S. citizens anticipate and approach national problems such as social or environmental problems. As outlined in a speech by U.S. Department of Commerce Secretary Don Evans to the Detroit Economic Club, September 15, 2003, U.S. industry and manufacturing have meant far more to U.S. citizens than just economic enterprise. As Mr. Evans pointed out, industry and manufacturing are part of the national identity.

> Americans are pioneers and inventors and visionaries. We built railroads and the telegraph to connect cities. We built automobiles and airplanes to give our citizens mobility. We built Liberty Ships to defeat tyranny. We built Apollo to reach the Moon. And in countless other variations spanning every sphere of life, American products help people around the world lead safer, healthier, and more satisfying lives. Americans working in the spirit of Franklin, Bell, Deere, Edison, Ford, Dell, and Gates have transformed the world and raised global living standards.

Thus, when Americans have designed solutions to social or environmental challenges, such as improving the education of children or improving the environment, they have

Figure 6—Growth in U.S. industrial production on a monthly basis (year-over-year), and monthly U.S. industrial capacity utilization (Federal Reserve 2006a).

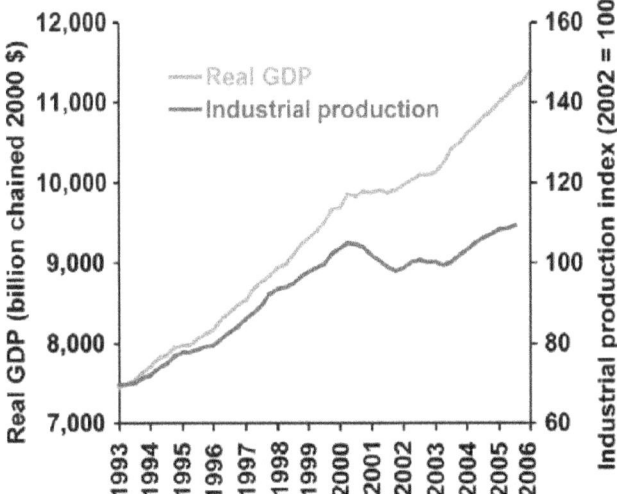

Figure 7—Real U.S. gross domestic product (billions, 2000 U.S. dollars) and quarterly U.S. industrial production index, 1993–2005 (BEA 2004; Federal Reserve 2006a). 1975–1999, $p = 0.98$; 2000–2004, $p = -0.38$.

resorted to technological solutions. For example, in primary and secondary education, classroom use of computers, televisions, recording devices, visual aids, and other modern technologies have become synonymous with improving the education process. Likewise, use of automotive emission control devices and fuel efficiency improvements have become synonymous with reduced air pollution and resource conservation. In general, Americans have invoked industrial or technological solutions to sustainable development problems, and until recently that approach was reinforced by positive correlation between two key economic indicators, GDP and industrial output. Industry and technology were part of the national identity essentially because industrial output was correlated to broader economic growth and prosperity, but in recent years that correlation was offset by structural changes in the overall economy. Measures of sustainable forest management such as the Montréal Process Criteria and Indicators (discussed later), however, assert that many environmental and social elements of well being are not fully accounted for in the GDP model (but require various additional bio-physical measures).

Figure 7 shows quarterly trends over recent years in U.S. GDP (BEA 2004) and the overall U.S. industrial production index (Federal Reserve 2006a). Historically, U.S. industrial output and GDP were positively correlated and only slowly diverging (as the service sector expanded historically). However, that divergence widened significantly in the late 1990s as the U.S. trade deficit in goods expanded to record proportions and as manufacturing output peaked in the year 2000 and then declined. Whereas historically there was a strong positive correlation between quarterly U.S. industrial production and GDP growth (correlation coefficient, $p = +0.98$ from 1975 to 1999), that positive correlation disappeared for a period, replaced by a negative correlation ($p = -0.32$ from 2000 through 2003). After 2003, positive correlation reemerged, but the two indicators continued to diverge from one another (Fig. 7).

Similarly, U.S. timber harvest has diverged from broader GDP growth, and evidence indicates that an ongoing decline in timber harvest relative to GDP was accelerated along with globalization and consolidation since the early 1990s. United States timber harvest was gradually diverging from GDP growth for most of the last century, but since 1991 U.S. timber harvest declined at a much more rapid pace relative to GDP. Figure 8 illustrates the trend from 1975 to 2002 in U.S. timber harvest relative to GDP. United States timber harvest per million dollars of real GDP declined by 11% in the period from 1975 to 1991, but then from 1991 to 2002 it declined by 38%, as economic globalization affected the forest sector. The accelerated decline in timber harvest per million dollars of GDP since the early 1990s coincides with noted shifts in various indicators of economic globalization, such as the record expansion of the U.S. goods trade deficit (Fig. 3), structural displacement of labor in manufacturing (Fig. 1), and a broader disconnect between overall U.S. industrial output and GDP growth (Fig. 7).

Recent history suggests also that alternative approaches to sustainable forest management can gain ascendancy over economic or technological approaches if connections between forest industry development and broader economic prosperity become diminished. For example, until the 1980s much of the timberland in the National Forest System was available for scheduled timber harvest under the management discretion of the USDA Forest Service, applying the policy of nondeclining even flow to ensure sustainable timber supplies (Fedkiw 1997). National forests of the U.S. Pacific Northwest (PNW) region were among the leading sources of timber in the mid-20th century, up until the late 1980s. However, the late 1980s to early 1990s was a period of transition in national forest management, as political concerns arose in the PNW region about protecting old-growth Douglas-fir on the national forests as habitat for endangered

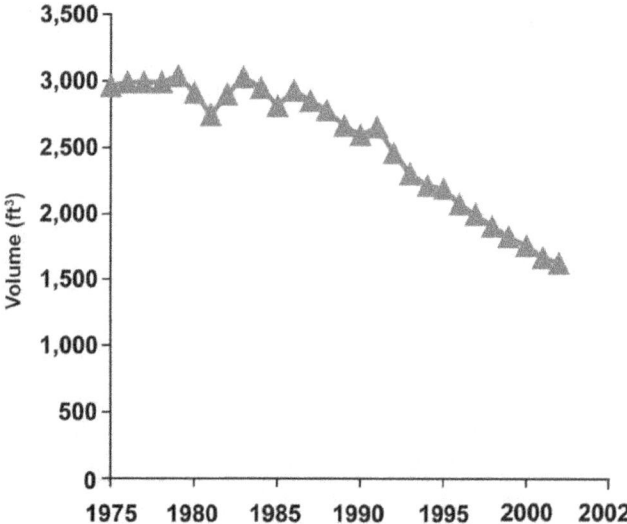

Figure 8—United States timber harvest volume (ft³) per million dollars of real gross domestic product (2000 U.S. dollars), 1975–2002.

species such as the northern spotted owl. By the 1980s, economic development and job growth in the PNW region had also shifted from the forest sector to other economic sectors, although many local forest product mills remained dependent on timber from the national forests. The Forest Service estimated that during the period of transition approximately 31,000 jobs were lost in the forest sector in Washington and Oregon as national forest timber harvest was reduced, but 866,000 jobs were created in other economic sectors within those states during the same period. The employment figures suggest a practical reason why economic or technological approaches did not come to play a central role in local resolution of sustainable forest policy issues at that time: the public identity with the forest sector as a source of jobs, prosperity, and developing technology had become subordinated in the context of broader economic development and other technological sources of economic prosperity. Other forest management approaches gained ascendancy, replacing forest management approaches that were based previously on economic considerations or technological needs of the forest product industry.

Industrial and technological solutions definitely played a role at the national level in coping with declining timber supply from public forests in the West, with development of OSB production in the U.S. East replacing plywood production in the West, expansion in the area and productivity of Southern Pine plantations in the U.S. South, a shift to Southern Pine lumber production, and increased paper recycling. In addition, imports of softwood lumber and OSB from Canada increased, and softwood log exports from the West Coast declined. Those developments offset the negative effects of declining harvest of Douglas-fir and other timber species in the PNW region.

However, at the local level within the PNW region, a set of judicial and regulatory solutions played a primary role in resolving public forest management issues within the region, rather than economic or technological solutions per se. This is not to say that technological or economic solutions would have worked better or worse than judicial or regulatory solutions. Rather, the point is simply that the local resolution of public policy issues could largely bypass technological and economic issues because the relative importance of the forest industry in the regional economy was rapidly diminishing. Public identity with forestry and resource management was diminishing because of structural changes in the local economy—through expansion of economic activity, technology, and employment in other sectors of the economy. Whereas many people were attracted to the PNW region by forest amenity values, which they wanted to preserve, their economic welfare was not directly connected to forest technology or resource management.

Likewise, ongoing structural changes in industrial production and forest sector growth in the current era of economic globalization may further shape the American identity and influence how U.S. citizens chart their pathway toward sustainable forest management in the future. History suggests that if the relative economic importance of forest industry, forestry technology, or forest product manufacturing continues to become diminished locally relative to other economic enterprises, then technological or industrial solutions to sustainable forest management may tend to give way to political, judicial, or regulatory solutions, as in the PNW region in the late 1980s.

In other parts of the world where forest industry retains a stronger connection to economic prosperity and national identity, most notably in Scandinavia, technological solutions seem to play a more central role in resolving sustainable forest management issues (such as with recent Scandinavian development of more modern timber harvest technology and harvest systems that leave a much lighter environmental footprint in forest ecosystems). In general, a further disconnect between U.S. GDP growth and industrial output, or between GDP growth and forest sector growth will likely shift the future pathway of sustainable development farther away from technological solutions toward other political, regulatory, or judicial solutions, which may not be favorable toward U.S. forest industry or its global competitiveness.

Effects of Economic Globalization on Society and the Environment

In addition to effects of economic globalization on local development opportunities, some empirical evidence supports a view that structural change and shifts in wealth arising from free trade and economic globalization have broad effects on society and the environment. In the literature on trade liberalization and the environment, those effects have been subdivided into three main categories, including technique effect, scale effect, and composition effect, described as follows (Nimon and others 2002):

Technique Effect. Trade liberalization results in shifts in technology, and thus may have a "technique effect" on society or the environment as producers adopt either dirtier or cleaner production technologies, whichever is more efficient, but cleaner technology appears to be favored as per capita wealth increases.

Scale Effect. Empirical evidence links trade liberalization to economic growth and expansion in scale of production. Increased output and scale of production resulting from trade liberalization may, however, generate additional pollution emissions or accelerate depletion of natural resources.

Composition Effect. Trade liberalization may affect composition of product output, such that resources devoted formerly to inefficient industries will be utilized more efficiently (for example, through the use of more capital- or skill-intensive means of production in the United States).

These observed effects support the environmental Kuznets curve idea, an inverted-U shaped relationship between environmental degradation and income, which suggests that environmental effects first increase but then decrease with increasing per capita income (as scale effects of dirtier technologies increase environmental burdens but eventually positive technique and composition effects reduce environmental burdens) (World Bank 1999). The environmental Kuznets curve is an extension of the classical Kuznets curve hypothesis regarding income inequality, advanced in 1955 by the economist Simon Kuznets. According to that hypothesis, income inequality first increases but then recedes with economic development (as a result of structural change in the economy). Although some empirical evidence exists for Kuznets curves, it is statistically weak or has been challenged by other studies that reject the Kuznets hypotheses, particularly the Kuznets income-inequality curve (Ravallion and Chen 1997).

The Kuznets curve hypotheses are controversial, and in some cases contradicted by data, but nevertheless the environmental effects of income or prosperity are relevant topics to consider in relation to economic globalization, along with technique, scale, and composition effects. In the U.S. forest sector, for example, the scale effect may actually be reversed in regard to wood resource utilization, as the larger scale and more capital-intensive pulp and paper mills tend to use wood resources the most efficiently, with little or no wood waste and high rates of wood fiber recycling (via paper recycling). In general, globalization and trade liberalization appear to affect the environment in a variety of ways, some positive and some negative (Nimon and others 2002). Also, the Kuznets curve suggests that promoting global acceptance of U.S. standards for worker safety, health, minimum wages, and environmental protection could be a strategic remedy to many of the challenges of economic globalization. However, before discussing strategic remedies in more detail, a more in-depth review of structural change is

needed to interpret more precisely the effects of economic globalization in the U.S. forest sector.

Structural Change in Forest Product Markets

The following sections provide a more in-depth overview of how economic globalization has contributed to structural change and shifts in raw material markets in the U.S. forest product sector, considering developments in pulp and paper, furniture and hardwood lumber, softwood lumber and housing, and the wood panels sector.

Pulp and Paper

Economic globalization and structural change appear to have deeply affected the pattern of growth in the U.S. pulp and paper sector in recent years. The United States is still by far the leading global producer of pulp, paper, and paperboard products. However, U.S. output of paper and paperboard peaked in the year 1999 and subsequently declined through the year 2003. United States wood pulp output peaked earlier, in the mid-1990s and also subsequently declined. The recent declines in U.S. pulp, paper, and paperboard output are the largest and most prolonged declines in the history of U.S. pulping and papermaking, going all the way back to the 1800s. This section discusses several topics related to the recent declines in U.S. pulp, paper, and paperboard output: (1) How globalization influenced economic trends of the pulp and paper sector in recent years; (2) How these trends influenced the supply and demand outlook for pulpwood and wood fiber in the United States; and (3) What the direct implications are for forest management and forest resource conditions.

Influence of Economic Globalization

Economic globalization and record levels of goods imports contributed to a leveling out and decline of U.S. industrial production from 2000 to 2003 (Figs. 1–5), and that decline also deeply affected pulp, paper, and paperboard demand. Paper and paperboard products serve many markets, but there are three principal end uses: packaging, communication, and sanitary products. The largest end use is packaging, where paper and paperboard are used for retail packaging and for shipping containers (such as corrugated boxes). The next largest end use is the use of paper for communication in print media, advertising, publishing, business, and education. The packaging and communication end uses are both closely tied to the overall level of business and manufacturing activity in the U.S. economy, via packaging and shipping of most goods in commerce and via the use of paper for print advertising and business applications. In print media such as newspapers and magazines, the bulk of revenues are generated by business and product advertising expenditures. Thus, the recent downturn in U.S. industrial output (Fig. 6) contributed also to a significant downturn in domestic paper and paperboard demand, particularly in packaging and print advertising. Demand for tissue and sanitary paper products remained relatively steady, but

Figure 9—United States paper and paperboard production (6-month moving average, AF&PA 2006) and growth in overall U.S. industrial production (Federal Reserve 2006a).

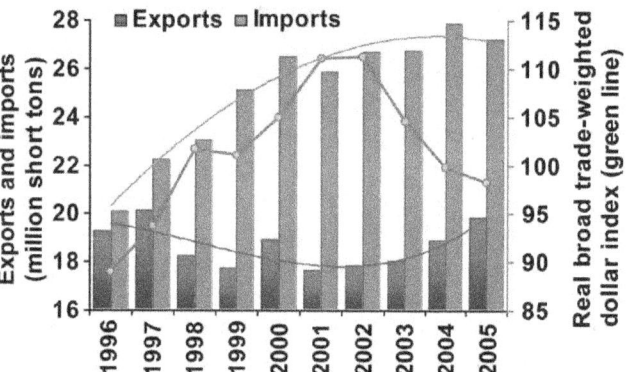

Figure 10—The green line (dollar index) indicates trends in total annual U.S. exports and imports of pulp, paper, and paperboard products, and real broad trade-weighted dollar index, 1996–2005. Data include paper and paperboard products and wood pulp shipment (AF&PA 2006; Federal Reserve 2006).

demand for tissue and sanitary paper is small relative to packaging and communication grades of paper and paperboard (just 8% of U.S. production in 2003). Figure 9 illustrates that monthly U.S. paper and paperboard production has tracked fairly closely the recent downturn of growth in overall U.S. industrial output (measured by the year-over-year change in the Federal Reserve monthly index of U.S. industrial production).

United States paper and paperboard domestic purchases also peaked in 1999 and then declined along with declining growth in overall industrial production, as demands for paper and paperboard in packaging and print advertising receded. Thus, U.S. paper and paperboard demand along with overall manufacturing output were deeply affected by economic globalization. Industrial output has increased since 2001, and a bumpy upturn has been under way also for paper and paperboard output (Fig. 9), but the recent downturn was quite severe, and full recovery to previous

peak levels will likely take some time. By 2006, paper and paperboard output still remained about 5% below peak levels of the late 1990s.

Furthermore, with a surge in the real exchange value of the U.S. dollar from 1996 to 2002, U.S. markets were flooded by pulp and paper imports from Europe and Canada, as well as from Asia and Latin America, and also U.S. exports of finished pulp, paper, and paperboard products declined. In total tonnage, the U.S. trade deficit in pulp, paper, and paperboard products soared from less than 1 million tons of net imports in 1996 to around 9 million tons of net imports in 2003, with trade influenced by the strong U.S. dollar. Figure 10 shows the recent historical trend in annual U.S. exports and imports of pulp, paper, and paperboard products (AF&PA 2006), along with the trend in the real trade-weighted dollar index (Federal Reserve 2006). The trade-weighted exchange value of the dollar declined from 2003 to 2005, and subsequently net imports of pulp, paper, and paperboard receded from 9 million tons to 7 million tons by 2005, and exports began to show signs of recovery (Fig. 10).

The recent decade-long divergence between U.S. exports and imports of pulp, paper, and paperboard began in 1997–1998 (Fig. 10), prior to the more recent decline in industrial production in 2000. This is partly attributable to loss of export markets during the so-called Asian financial crisis in the late 1990s. As currencies among some Asian countries were devalued, U.S. exports began to decline, and the United States began to experience a flood of imports, including imports from Europe as well as Asia.

Thus, since the mid-1990s, economic globalization had a two-fold effect on the pulp and paper sector, including (1) a downward effect on U.S. domestic demands for paper and paperboard in packaging and print advertising correlated with a downturn in U.S. industrial production stemming from record goods imports and structural changes in manufacturing and (2) a direct effect on pulp, paper, and paperboard trade, with loss of growth in exports and significant expansion of imports. Both effects were driven in part by the recent surge in the U.S. dollar value from 1996 to 2002, but other factors also contributed to competitive displacement of market share by imports and the loss of growth in U.S. exports. Those factors included wage rates, with rapid expansion of pulp and paper production capacity in lower income countries such as in Asia and Latin America, and wood cost, as pulp and paper producers in some parts of Asia and Latin America benefited from highly productive wood fiber plantations using fast-growing subtropical species such as eucalyptus or acacia.

Primary pulp, paper, or paperboard products, such as kraft market pulp, newsprint, linerboard, and various grades of printing and writing paper are sold as commodity products in the global market. This facilitates trade but also tends to limit opportunities for product differentiation. In addition, the differential between local and global shipping cost is relatively small (5% to 10% of product value).

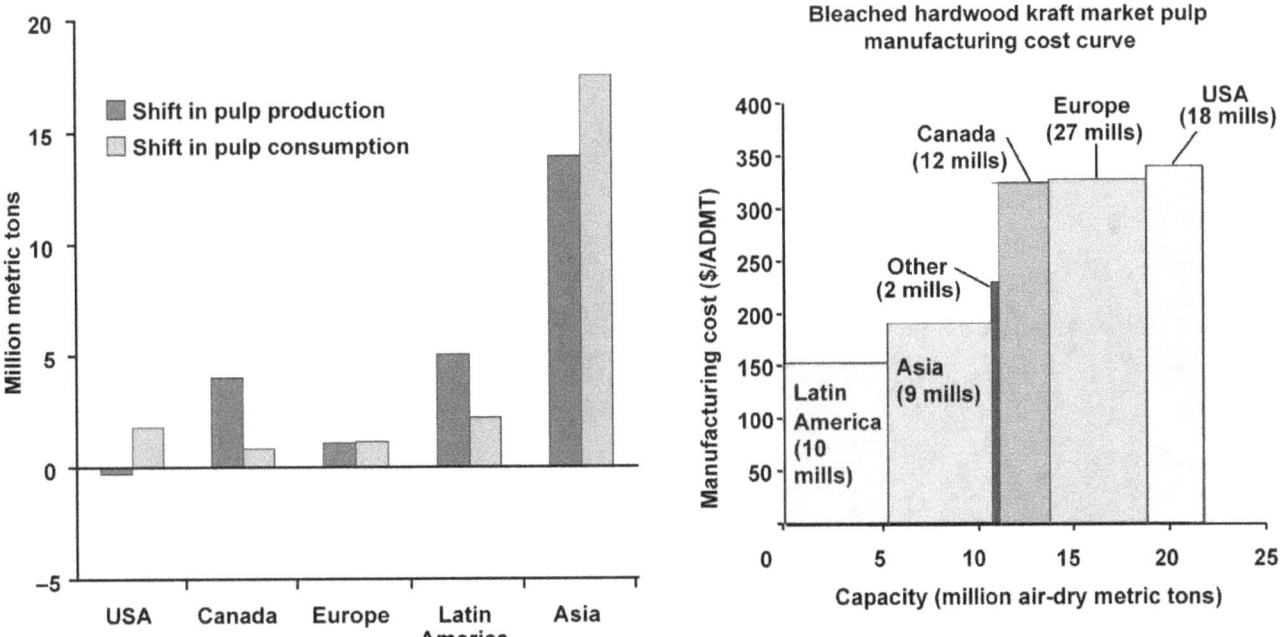

Figure 11—Global shifts in pulp production, 1990–2000, and 2002 global cost-capacity curve for hardwood market pulp producers. Left chart: PPI (2002). Right chart: NLK (2002). ADMT, air-dry metric ton.

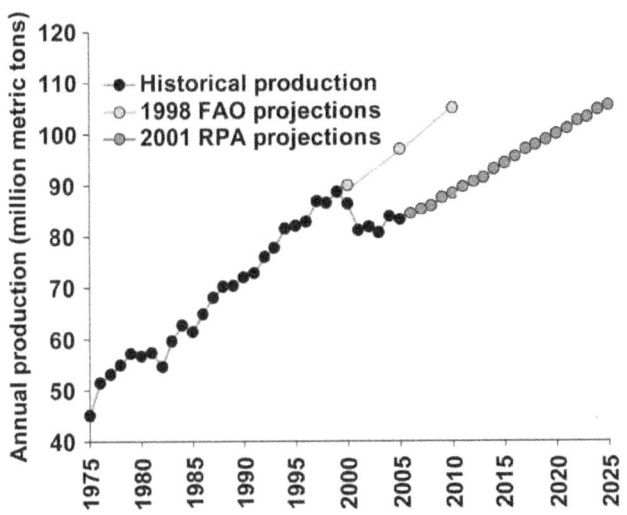

Figure 12—United States annual production of paper and paperboard, 1975–2005, along with 1998 FAO and Forest Service 2001 RPA projections (FAO 2001; Haynes 2003).

Consequently, competitiveness and global allocation of capacity growth are determined largely by production cost, as influenced by wage rates, costs of fiber raw material, and currency exchange rates. Other factors also play a role, such as availability of capital for mill investments, energy costs, corporate tax rates, regulatory compliance, timeliness of product delivery, and so forth.

In the 1990s, growth in pulp output shifted from Europe and North America to Asia and Latin America, a trend favored by lower production costs and wood fiber from fast-growing plantations. Figure 11 shows shifts in pulp production and consumption among global regions during the decade of the 1990s, along with 2002 costs and capacities for hardwood market pulp (hardwood kraft) among global regions. Throughout the 1990s Asia and Latin America had far more growth in pulp production than all other regions, mostly hardwood pulp, with mill investments lured to those regions by low production costs. By 2002, pulp producers in Latin America and Asia had a big advantage in production costs, with lower wages, lower fiber costs, and larger new mills. A weaker U.S. dollar since 2002 has narrowed but has not eliminated the cost advantage.

Although global pulp production trends in the 1990s pointed to other regions as the locus of growth in pulp and paper output, the decline in U.S. paper and paperboard output since 1999 was nevertheless an abrupt departure from historical trends. Through the 1990s, U.S. paper and paperboard output continued to increase fairly steadily, even though exports began to recede in 1997 and U.S. wood pulp output peaked in the mid-1990s. Thus, as late as 1998 economic projections of U.S. paper and paperboard production showed continued expansion of output into the 21st century, as exemplified by projections developed for the Food and Agriculture Organization (FAO) of the United Nations (FAO 1998). Shortly after the 1998 FAO projections were made, U.S. paper and paperboard output peaked and subsequently declined, as shown in Figure 12. Also shown in Figure 12 are projections of U.S. paper and paperboard production made in 2001 for the Forest Service RPA timber assessment (Haynes 2003).

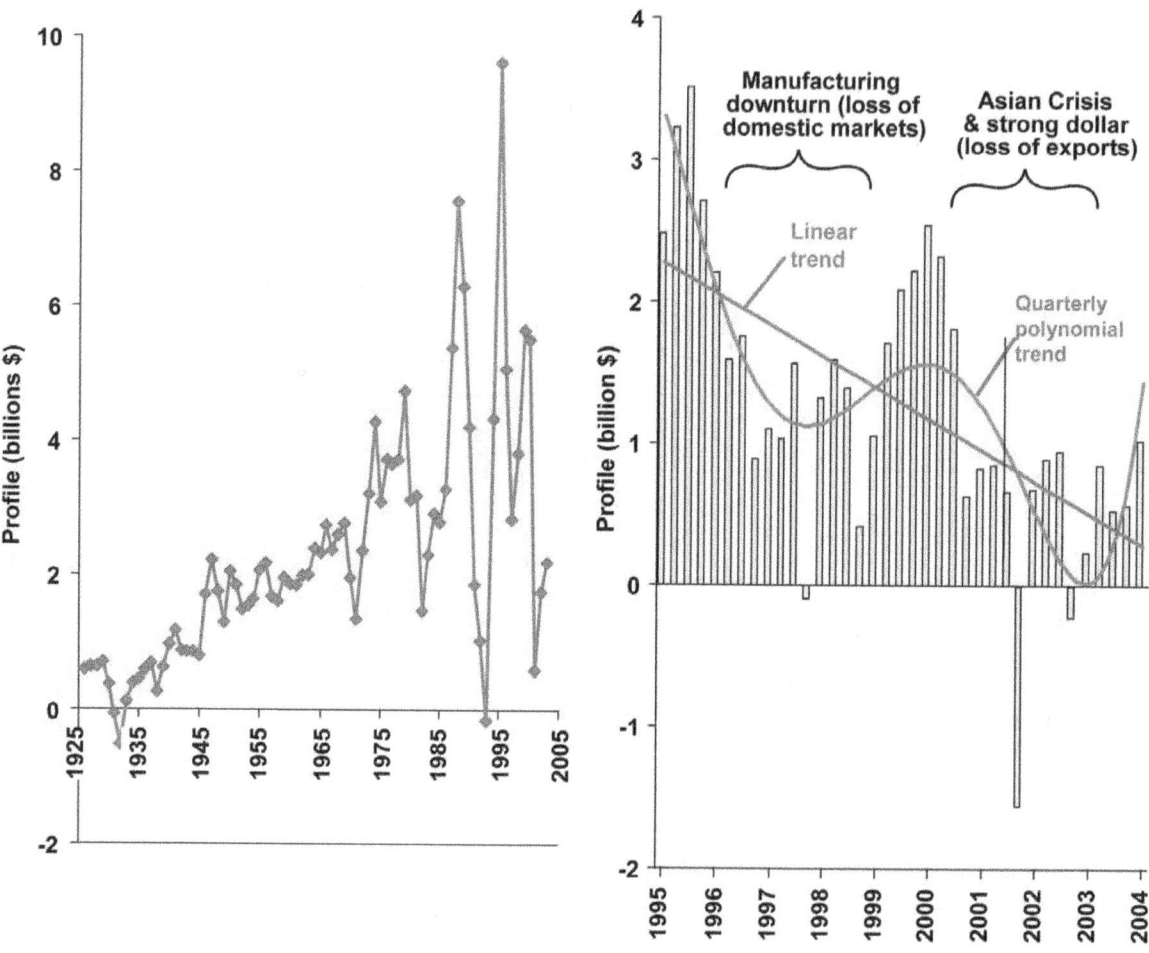

Figure 13—After-tax profits of U.S. paper and allied products industry, real annual basis 1925–2004 (1982 dollars), and quarterly nominal basis, as reported (U.S. Department of Commerce 2006; U.S. Department of the Treasury 2006; AF&PA 2006).

The RPA projections indicated that growth would return to U.S. paper and paperboard output, but there was a large gap between the 2001 RPA projections and FAO projections made three years earlier, with FAO projections for 2010 not being reached until 2025 according to RPA. Thus, the recent downturn in U.S. paper and paperboard output pointed to a significant departure from historical trends.

Moreover, declining paper and paperboard output reflected a significant decline over the past decade in industry profits. As illustrated in Figure 13, after-tax profits of the U.S. paper and allied products industry generally declined after peaking in the mid-1990s, in a downturn that dwarfed the industry profit decline of the Great Depression in the 1930s. Volatility and steep declines in industry profits occurred during rapid global capacity expansion in the early 1990s, during the Asian crisis of the late 1990s (with loss of growth in U.S. exports), and during the recent U.S. manufacturing downturn from 2000 to 2002. Profits were improving in 2003–2004, but are still low by historical standards.

As production waned and paper industry profits spiraled downward from 1995 to 2002, more than 90 U.S. pulp, paper, or paperboard mills were shut down (mostly older or less efficient mills), with numerous other partial mill closures. Industry capacity expansion ground to a halt, and capital investment declined sharply. Total production capacity of U.S. paper and paperboard mills receded in the year 2001 for the first time in many decades (Fig. 14) and continued to recede in 2002 to 2006, with very little capacity growth anticipated in the next couple of years (AF&PA 2002).

Annual capital expenditures at U.S. pulp and paper mills dropped by more than one-third between 1996 and 2002, falling below annual depreciation levels (Census Bureau 2002a). The decline in capital spending reduced optimism about long-term competitiveness. Some 48% of surveyed mill managers in 2002 believed that their company was not investing sufficient capital in their mill to retain its competitiveness (Paperloop 2002). The vital role of capital investment in maintaining industry competitiveness is clearly recognized by industry experts (Kinstrey 2004).

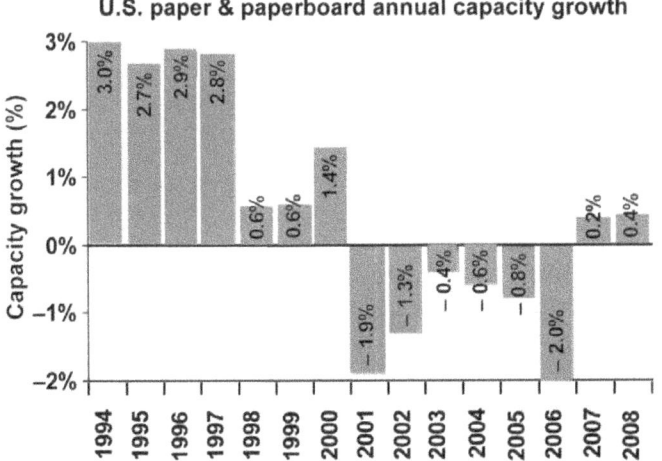

Figure 14—Decline in capacity growth for U.S. paper and paperboard mils, with little projected growth (AF&PA 2006).

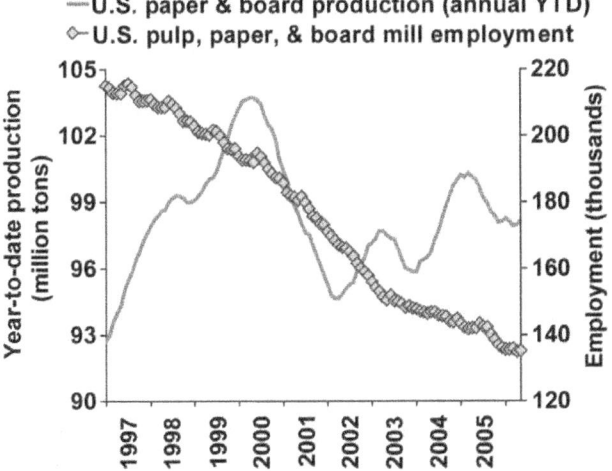

Figure 15—Decline in U.S. pulp, paper, and paperboard mill employment associated with recent downturn in U.S. paper and paperboard production, 1997–2005. Employment, BLS (2006); production, AF&PA (2006).

Capital spending at leading U.S. pulp and paper firms increased modestly in 2003 to 2005 as markets improved with the upturn in industrial production, but capital spending still remained well below historical peak levels of previous decades.

With consolidation, downsizing, and a push toward lower costs and higher productivity, significant job losses were recorded in the pulp and paper sector, particularly at pulp, paper, and paperboard mills. Total employments at U.S. pulp, paper, and paperboard mills dropped by around 80,000 from 1997 to 2005 (BLS 2006), a loss of about one out of every three jobs at mills since January 1997. Figure 15 shows the decline in U.S. pulp, paper, and paperboard mill employment from 1997 through 2005, which was associated over that period with the peaking and downturn in U.S. paper and paperboard production. Although production

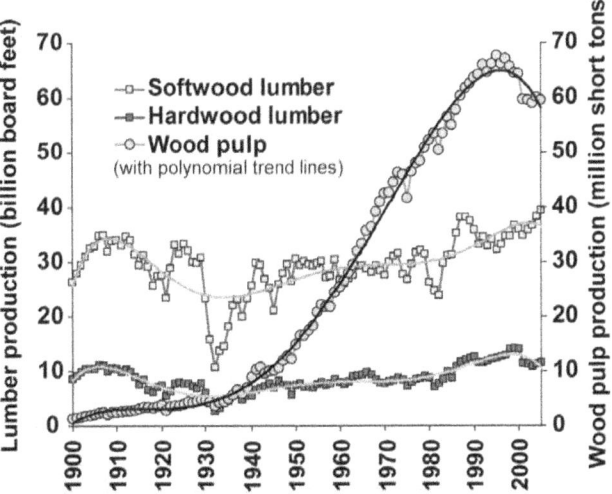

Figure 16—United States annual production of lumber and wood pulp, 1900–2005. Wood pulp includes estimates of dissolving pulp and wood pulp for construction paper and board (FS 2003, AF&PA 2006, Hardwood Review 2004).

dropped by just less than 10% from its peak in 1999 to its low point in 2002, mill employment dropped by over 30% from 1997 to 2005, as many smaller and more labor-intensive operations were shut down.

Influence on Fiber Supply and Demand Outlook

Economic globalization and structural change in paper and paperboard markets contributed to an historic shift in U.S. wood pulp output and pulpwood demand since the mid-1990s. Throughout most of the 20th century, U.S. wood pulp output climbed steadily with paper and paperboard output, becoming the leading end use of wood and wood fiber in the economy (taking into account use of wood residues and roundwood pulpwood). The growth of U.S. wood pulp output up to the mid-1990s was remarkable because of its consistent upward trend, which was generally much less variable than other major end uses for wood such as hardwood or softwood lumber, for example. Figure 16 illustrates growth over the past century in annual U.S. wood pulp production along with trends in production of hardwood and softwood lumber. Although the recent decline in wood pulp output is proportionately smaller than historical declines in lumber production, nevertheless the drop in wood pulp output since the mid-1990s is by far the biggest downturn for wood pulp of the past century—bigger than any other decline in the history of wood pulp production (more than declines in the Great Depression of the 1930s or in the energy crisis of the 1970s). Increased paper recycling in the late 1980s and early 1990s played a role in leveling out growth of U.S. wood pulp output, as the recovered paper utilization rate increased from 24% in 1985 to 37% in 1996, but utilization of recycled fiber has not increased significantly since then (reaching just 38% in 2002) AF&PA (2003). Most of the decline in wood pulp output occurred more recently

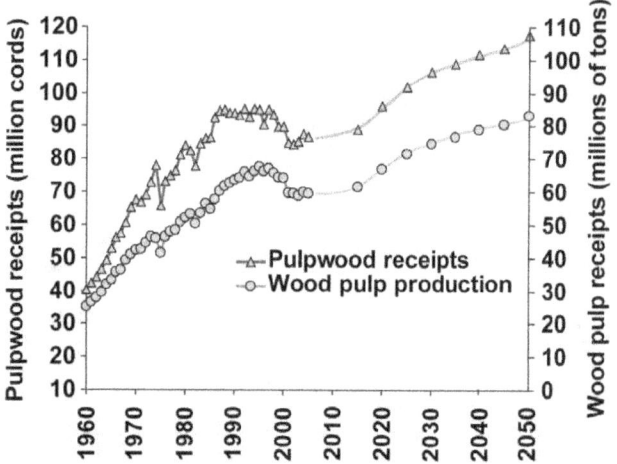

Figure 17—United States annual pulpwood receipts at wood pulp mills and wood pulp production, 1960–2005, with RPA projections to 2050. Projections, Forest Service RPA (Haynes 2003); historical pulpwood, (FRA 2003); historical wood pulp (AF&PA 2006).

when paper and paperboard output peaked in 1999 and then declined (Fig. 12), along with industry consolidation and the recent downturn of growth in overall U.S. manufacturing (Fig. 6).

The downturn in U.S. pulp and paper output was recognized and taken into account in the previous Forest Service RPA timber assessment (Haynes 2003). The analysis of the pulp and paper sector for the timber assessment was done in 2001, and the analysis projected that the downturn in wood pulp output would be prolonged well into the current decade, reaching a low point around mid-decade and then recovering in the years ahead along with an anticipated upturn in paper and paperboard demand (Fig. 12). The 2001 RPA analysis still appears reasonably accurate in light of more recent trends, with an upturn for paper and paperboard output in 2004. The historical data and RPA analysis indicate nevertheless that U.S. wood pulp production made a significant departure since the early 1990s from its historical trend (Fig. 16), and likewise there was a significant departure from historical trends in nationwide pulpwood demand.

Figure 17 illustrates historical trends and the 2001 RPA projections for U.S. wood pulp output and pulpwood receipts at wood pulp mills. After declining from peak levels of the mid-1990s to a projected low point in the current decade, the RPA projections show a gradual recovery for wood pulp production and pulpwood receipts at wood pulp mills, but nevertheless full recovery is projected to take decades. Thus the recent downturn and projected trends indicate an enormous displacement of growth in pulpwood demands relative to the growth trends of the 1960s to early 1990s.

The downturn in pulpwood demand was a significant structural change in the overall U.S. timber demand situation, particularly in regions where continued growth in pulpwood demand had been anticipated or where forest management

was expected to benefit from increased pulpwood use. Since peaking in 1994 at 265 million green tons (including roundwood and residues), U.S. pulpwood receipts at wood pulp mills declined by just over 15% to 222 million green tons in 2002 (FRA 2003).

Over that period, pulpwood receipts at wood pulp mills in the U.S. South also declined by just over 15% from a peak of 200 million green tons in 1994 to 168 million in 2002 (FRA 2003). Ironically, the South is the largest pulpwood producing region of the country (with the largest share of capacity for pulp, paper, and paperboard) and the South was a region that had anticipated expansion in pulpwood demand up to the mid-1990s with expansion in the area and intensity of pine plantations, but nevertheless the decline in pulpwood receipts in the South matches (in percentage terms) the nationwide decline.

A more significant decline in pulpwood demand occurred in the West, with pulpwood receipts dropping by 28% from their peak of 32 million green tons in 1995 to 23 million in 2002 (FRA 2003). The decline in the West is problematic given needs to increase thinning and removal of small-diameter timber for fire hazard reduction in the West.

Pulpwood receipts declined significantly in the Northeast, by 31% from a peak of 19 million tons in 1994 to 13 million in 2002, with closure of a number of older mills in that region. In the North Central (Lake States) region, pulpwood receipts peaked at 19 million green tons in 1994 and then declined, but the net decline in that region between 1994 and 2002 was only 7%, to 18 million green tons in 2002 (FRA 2003).

Implications for Forest Management and Resource Conditions

Globalization, recycling, and the downturn in pulpwood demand contributed to fundamentally changing the RPA outlook for timber harvest and forest resource conditions in the United States (e.g., projected timber growing stock volumes). Until the early 1990s, the trend in wood pulp output pointed unambiguously toward increasing pulpwood demand (Fig. 17). Economic advantages of paper recycling and potential effects of shifts in trade were recognized by the late 1980s, but the baseline RPA outlook of that time conformed to the historical trend in wood pulp output. Many doubted then that recycling or shifts in trade could cause a real departure from the historical trend. However, after taking into account recent structural changes in pulpwood markets, including higher rates of recycling and effects of economic globalization, projected pulpwood receipts at wood pulp mills were roughly 50 million cords per year lower in the 2001 RPA than in the 1989 RPA timber assessment, as shown in Figure 18. Furthermore, supplies of wood residues for pulpwood were expected to level out or decline, with increased lumber recovery efficiency and with a shift from wood products that generate wood chip residues, such as plywood, to products that do not generate wood chip

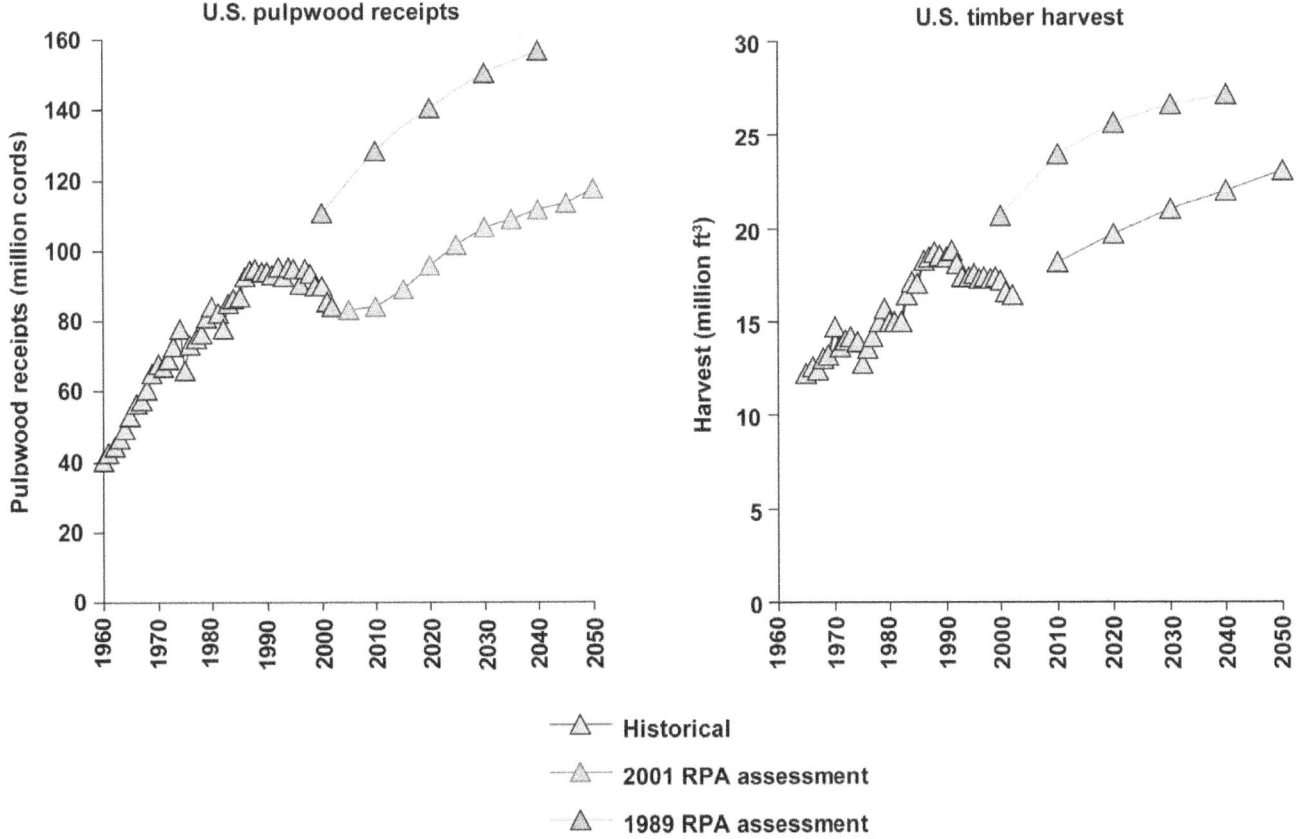

Figure 18—Trends in U.S. pulpwood receipts and total U.S. timber harvest—historical and comparison of 2001 and 1989 RPA equilibrium projections. Historical trend in harvest based on estimated roundwood equivalents of production (Howard 2003a, b).

residues, such as OSB. Therefore, most of the downward adjustment in pulpwood demand translated directly into reduced projections of roundwood pulpwood harvest.

As shown in Figure 18, projected annual U.S. timber harvest was 5 to 6 billion ft³ lower in the 2001 RPA than in the 1989 RPA, and most of that adjustment in projected timber harvest was the result of the downward adjustment in projected pulpwood demand, equivalent to roughly 4 billion ft³ per year. The remainder of the harvest adjustment is attributable to a downward revision in projected fuel wood demand, while projections of wood use in lumber and wood panels were changed very little.

As shown in Figure 18, the 2001 RPA projections for pulpwood receipts are fairly close to the historical trend for pulpwood receipts, but recent data on total timber harvest now appear slightly lower than the RPA projections of total timber harvest, perhaps because of additional unanticipated negative effects of globalization in other forest product sectors, notably in furniture and the hardwood lumber sector as discussed subsequently in this report. Nevertheless, the large adjustments that were made to projected pulpwood demand in the 2001 RPA timber assessment (along with other smaller adjustments) contributed to significantly changing the overall forest resource outlook, including the outlook for

the overall condition and sustainability of timber growing stock volumes in the United States.

Historically, U.S. timber growing stock volume has increased, and future timber growing stock volume was projected in the 2001 RPA to continue increasing, largely because of relatively modest projected increases in timber harvest along with higher growth rates on managed timber plantations. Timber growing stock volume on all U.S. timberland increased historically by 40% in the second half of the 20th century (1952 to 2002), and growing stock volume was projected in the 2001 RPA timber assessment to continue increasing by another 40% in the first half of the 21st century (Fig. 19). A principal reason on the demand side for the robust U.S. timber inventory outlook is the recent decline in pulpwood demand, a direct result of the recent downturn in paper and paperboard output (linked to economic globalization), and also a result of increased paper recycling in the 1990s. In addition, the 2001 timber outlook reflects substantial improvement in tracking and modeling of timber growth and inventories on public forestlands between the 1989 and 2001 assessments.

Although slower growth in pulpwood demand was anticipated as early as the mid-1990s, the area and management intensity of Southern Pine plantations in the U.S. South

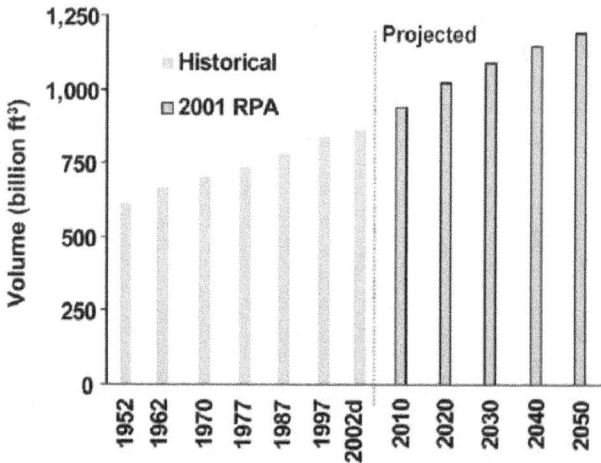

Figure 19—Total U.S. timber growing stock volume on all U.S. timberland—historical and comparison of RPA projections.

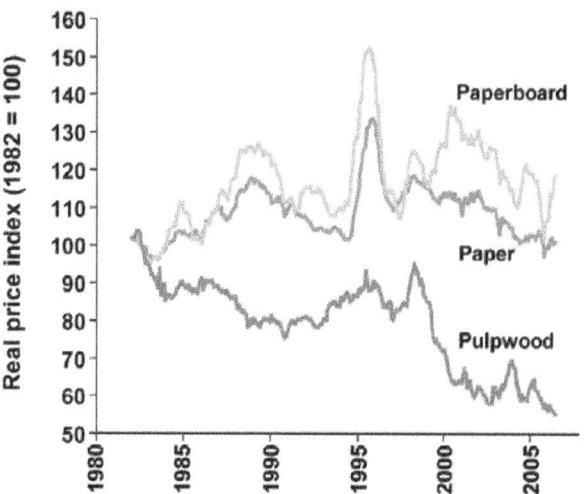

Figure 20—Real (inflation-adjusted) price indexes for paper, paperboard, and pulpwood (delivered to mill), 1982–2006 (BLS 2006, deflated using producer price index).

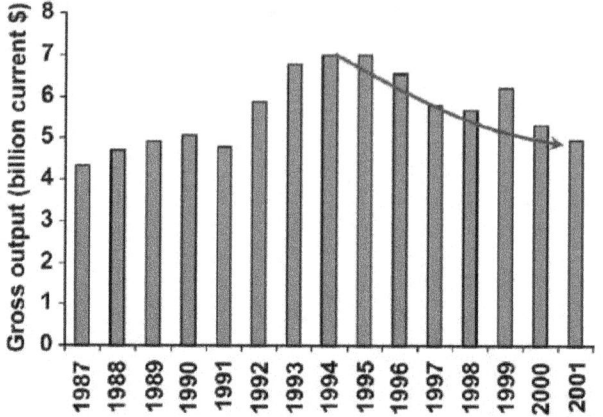

Figure 21—Gross output of forestry in the United States, in billions of current dollars, 1987–2001. Note 29% decline after U.S. pulpwood receipts peaked in 1994.

continued to increase through the 1990s. For example, while taking into account increased paper recycling, the 1993 RPA timber assessment update projected a trend for pulpwood receipts that was lower than the 1989 RPA, or roughly midway between projections of the 1989 and 2001 RPA (Fig. 18). Nevertheless, establishment of Southern Pine plantations actually accelerated from the 1980s to 1990s, with an estimated 32 million acres of Southern Pine planted in the South from 1985 to 2002 (including replanting and new plantation areas). The expansion of pine plantations contributed to excess pine pulpwood supply by the late 1990s as demand for pulpwood receded in the South while softwood timber inventories expanded.

In the U.S. South, softwood pulpwood receipts (mostly Southern Pine) peaked at 127 million green tons per year in the early 1990s, but then receded by 12% to

112 million green tons in 2002 (FRA 2003). By contrast, the average annual growth increment of Southern Pine plantations was estimated to have increased by 69 million green tons per year, between 1987 and 2004, the largest expansion of timber supply in modern U.S. history (Siry and Bailey 2003). Thus, growth in supply outpaced growth in demand, a market condition that was described in recent years as a glut in pine pulpwood supply (Minor 2002).

According to the South-wide average reported by Timber Mart-South (University of Georgia), Southern Pine pulpwood stumpage prices on average peaked around 1997 and declined to roughly half of their peak levels by 2002. Pine stumpage prices leveled out and turned upward slightly in 2003, but remained well below peak levels, and in real price terms near to historical lows. Nationwide, delivered pulpwood prices dropped on average by more than one-third since peaking in 1997, the most significant decline ever recorded by the Bureau of Labor Statistics producer price index for pulpwood. Figure 20 illustrates historical trends since the early 1980s in U.S. real price indexes for paper, paperboard, and pulpwood. In real price terms, U.S. pulpwood prices have been falling with expanding timber supply, but there was a record collapse in real pulpwood prices from 1997 to 2002. During that period, real price indexes for paper and paperboard also receded but did not collapse partly because of mill closures.

In summary, since the mid-1990s economic globalization and a downturn in U.S. industrial production contributed to a downturn in U.S. paper and paperboard demand, while a strong dollar contributed to loss of growth in U.S. pulp, paper, and paperboard exports and a flood of imports. These developments led to weak profits and structural changes in the pulp and paper sector, including consolidation, mill closures, reduced capital investment, reduced employment, and loss of growth in U.S. capacity. United States wood pulp production leveled out in the mid-1990s along with increased paper recycling and then declined along with

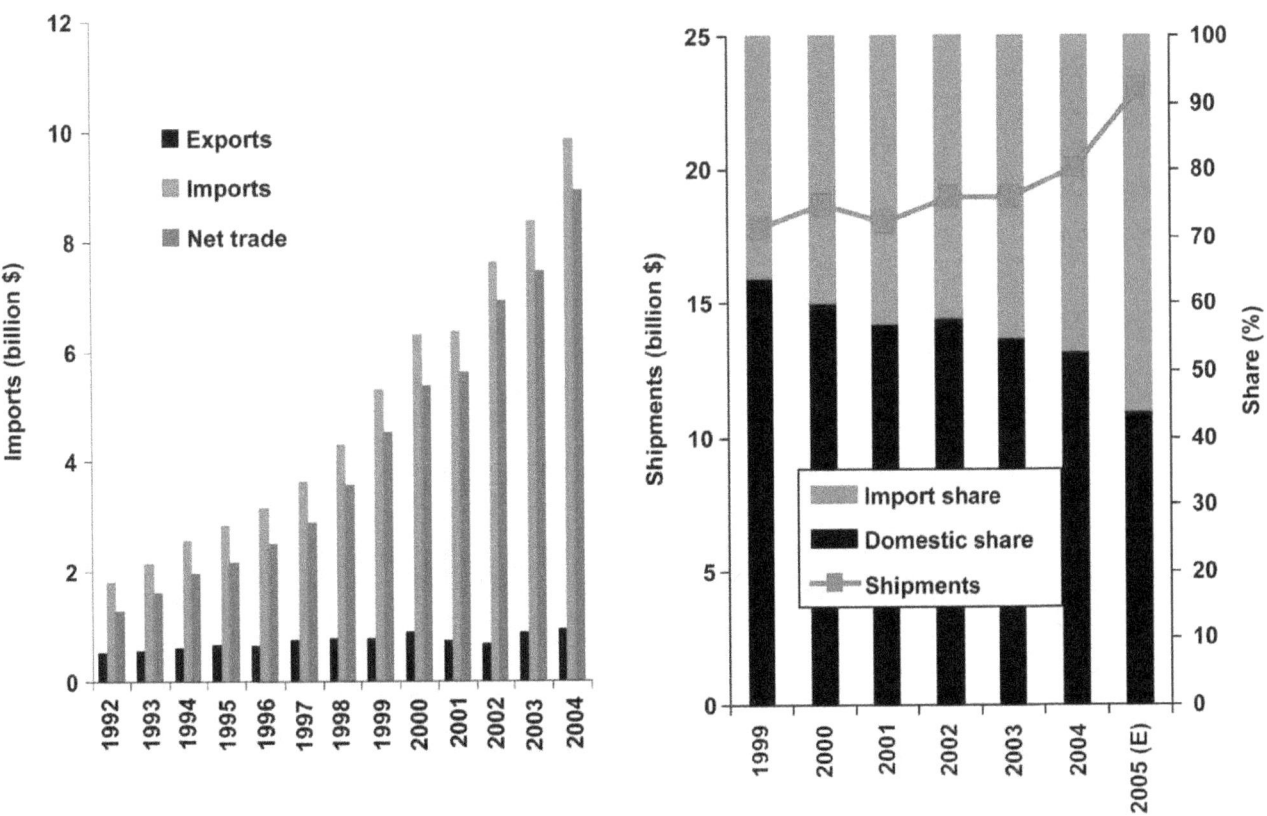

Figure 22—United States wood furniture imports escalated since the early 1990s as imports gained market share, showing the effects of globalization, NAFTA, WTO, and a strong dollar. Left graph shows wood nonupholstered household furniture: production data, (ASM 2006); import and export data, (ITA 2006). Right graph, (ITA 2006).

declining paper and paperboard output. Concurrently, pulpwood receipts at U.S. wood pulp mills peaked in the mid-1990s and subsequently declined, with an historic decline in real pulpwood prices. As projected in the 2001 RPA timber assessment, the recent downturn in pulpwood demand was sufficient to change the outlook for overall timber supply and demand in the United States and to influence the outlook for projected timber-growing stock volume in the United States.

Finally, gross economic output of forestry in the United States peaked in the year 1994, when U.S. pulpwood receipts peaked, and then subsequently declined, as pulpwood receipts and pulpwood prices declined. The gross output of forestry is an element of U.S. GDP (part of the forestry and agriculture component of the National Income and Product Accounts) (BEA 2002, 2004). As illustrated in Figure 21, the gross output of forestry dropped by 29% from 1994 to 2001, an economic trend that has only made it more challenging to gain support for forestry and forestry programs in the United States.

Furniture and Hardwood Lumber

In recent years, economic globalization also deeply affected the U.S. furniture industry, a major user of hardwood lumber and particleboard. United States imports of wood household

furniture went from around $2 billion in 1990 to nearly $10 billion by 2004, as shown in Figure 22. The imported share of U.S. wood furniture shipments went from under 20% before 1995 to over 50% by 2005. The value of shipments climbed 15% to more than $20 billion per year from 1999 to 2004, but the domestic share declined. Thus, U.S. demand for wood furniture was not declining in recent years, but rather the domestically produced market share and value of U.S. output declined in the face of rapidly expanding imports.

In recent years, Mainland China became the leading source of U.S. wood furniture imports, moving ahead of Canada. The United States and Canada reached a tariff reduction agreement in 1989, followed by signature of the North American Free Trade Agreement (NAFTA) in 1992. Canadian furniture producers made extensive investments to upgrade their plants, and thus gained competitive advantages in the 1990s. However, China's entry into the World Trade Organization (WTO) and its low wages gave China greater competitive advantages, and the Chinese furniture sector attracted large-scale foreign investment (FAS 2003). Thus, the flow of capital investment in furniture shifted to China and other low-income countries that accounted for most of the recent expansion in U.S. furniture imports. More than 50,000 furniture mills in China reportedly had output

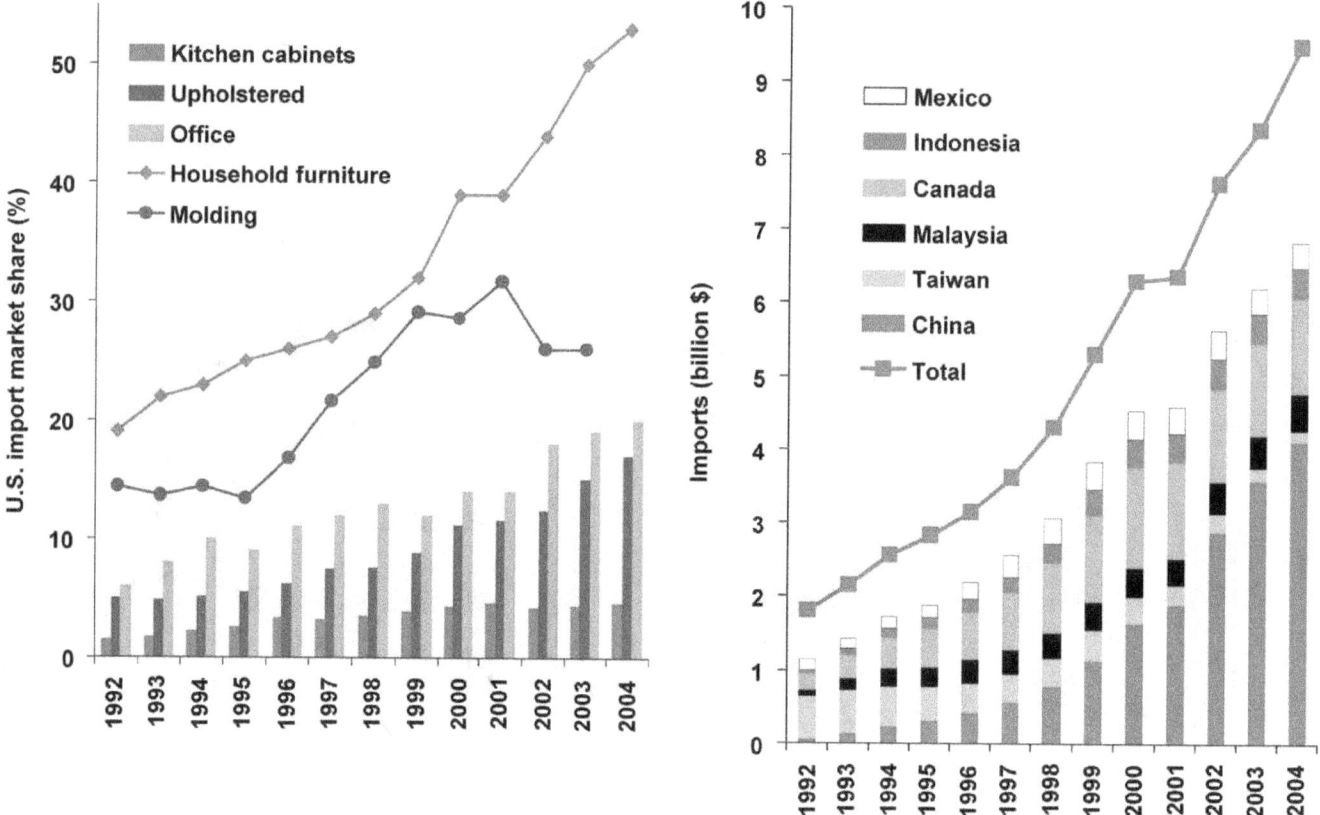

Figure 23—Wood household furniture imports and other furniture imports gaining market shares with growing imports from low-income countries, notably China. These market shares are conservative because some imported components and finished furniture are included in the domestic shipments. Consumption = shipments + imports – exports. Import share = imports/consumption (ASM 2006; Census Bureau 2006; ITA 2006).

of $19.8 billion in 2002, 18% higher than in 2001, and annual growth of 12% to 15% was expected in the years ahead (FAS 2003).

The phenomenon of overseas capacity expansion and expanding imports is spreading to other furniture products, like office and upholstered furniture, as shown by the import market share for various products in Figure 23. Most countries exporting furniture to the United States are low-wage countries, such as China, Malaysia, Indonesia, Mexico, and Vietnam, with Canada and Western European countries being exceptions. Another hardwood-based industry facing import competition is the flooring industry, particularly engineered wood flooring. Not surprisingly, much of this material is coming also from China. On a smaller scale, U.S. molding and millwork industries (both hardwood and softwood) have faced downsizing as a result of import competition, and many in the kitchen cabinet industry expect imports to make future inroads in wood cabinet markets also.

A social effect of these trends is a sharp drop in U.S. furniture industry employment, exemplified by the furniture industry employment trend for the state of North Carolina, shown in Figure 24. North Carolina was a major producer of wood household furniture, but nearly 40 North Carolina furniture plants were closed from 2001 to 2003, and the

negative furniture industry employment trends gained the attention of Congress. February 3, 2004, a forest subcommittee formed that examined job loss in the forest industry. The loss of furniture markets and jobs to imports in recent years is noteworthy because it happened during the strongest housing market in U.S. history (in terms of square feet of floor area and inflation-adjusted value of new home construction). Market conditions and housing trends created strong demands for new household furniture and kitchen cabinets, and by historical standards the employment and output of the furniture industry should have been increasing. Instead U.S. wood furniture industry declined in value of output and employment as market shares were lost to imports.

Important questions include the following: (1) Why have wood furniture and related U.S. hardwood industries declined with precipitous increases in imports? (2) What are implications for the "supply chain" of wood raw material to these industries? We refer chiefly to implications for hardwood lumber, particleboard, MDF (medium density fiberboard), and hardwood veneer industries, as well as related industries such as the pallet industry. (3) Are any effective solutions to these phenomena likely? If so, what are likely implications for sustainable forestry in general?

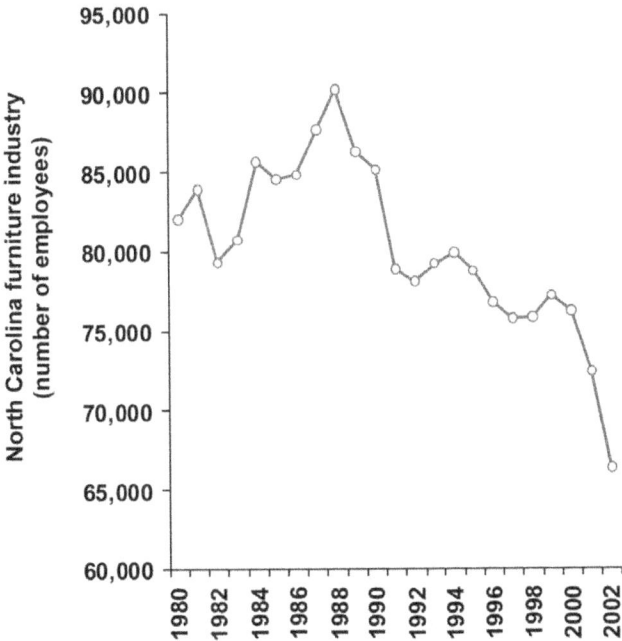

Figure 24—Furniture industry employment has fallen, gaining the attention of Congress.

One forestry ideal shared among many U.S. wood product firms today is sustainable forest management, meeting forest resource needs of both current and future generations by coordinating management of forest ecosystems with economic and social needs in a sustainable manner. Implicit to this ideal of sustainable forestry is the tenet that sustained management of forest resources requires sustained revenues, and in the private sector such revenues come primarily from the segments of the forest product industry that utilize outputs of forest ecosystems (primarily timber). This tenet of sustainable forestry is epitomized by a familiar forestry slogan, "healthy forests depend on a healthy forest product industry" (and vice versa). To those who are familiar with forestry in the largely private hardwood forest sector of the United States, it would appear that the one is predicated on the other. If the domestic hardwood industries—primary or secondary—lose their global competitiveness, what then are the sustainability implications for U.S. hardwood forests, land tenure, forest management, forest ecosystems, and so forth?

Why have wood furniture and related U.S. hardwood industries declined with precipitous increases in imports? The answer is neither simple nor straightforward, but the cost of labor is one critical factor influencing global patterns of capital investment in furniture production. Even with ambiguities in the data, it appears that wage rates and labor costs are key factors in how far the U.S. trade balance has shifted for furniture and related wood products. The data on household furniture imports, for example, do not include imports of wood furniture components, but those "hidden" furniture imports only add to displacement of wood raw material demands in furniture manufacture. Not only has

domestic furniture production been displaced by imports of finished furniture products, but also many U.S. furniture manufacturers have turned to imports of wooden furniture components, reportedly because of the lower costs. This is particularly true for the more labor-intensive wood furniture components such as carved furniture parts or other handcrafted items. Indeed, a business strategy commonly employed by U.S. furniture manufacturers to cope with competition from low-cost furniture imports is to reduce production costs by outsourcing components and increasing automation. Thus, the reported trade imbalance for wood furniture is conservative because it does not include all the imported wood furniture components coming into the United States. Moreover, despite the ambiguities in trade data, a structural change is definitely under way in the sourcing of both wood furniture and wood furniture components for U.S. markets, with a shift away from domestic production toward imports, driven by absolute cost advantages of countries with wage rates far below U.S. minimum wage standards.

Because wood furniture production is typically fairly labor-intensive, the advantage of production in low-wage countries can be quite substantial despite shipping costs and the possibility that workers in those countries are less productive than American workers. Wage rates at furniture plants in Mainland China, for example, were reportedly less than 5% of U.S. wage rates, with average earnings of $1,073 per year in 2002 (Banister 2005). Even though U.S. productivity per worker is typically higher, plants in China enjoy substantial competitive advantage in labor costs. For example, in the United States labor costs in the manufacture of wood household furniture may be typically around 35% of delivered cost (varying by type of furniture and manufacturer), while the cost of labor for similar furniture made in China may be only about 5% of the same delivered cost. In addition, energy costs tend to be slightly lower for manufacturers in China. This means that even though shipping costs from China are higher (amounting to about 15% of the cost), wood furniture made in China may enter U.S. markets with a profitable cost advantage of 30% or more primarily because of very low wage rates in China. Such cost advantage is a primary reason why China has attracted capital investment in furniture production.

Furthermore, demographic data indicate the U.S. population and work force is maturing, with a smaller share of workers in younger age cohorts. Figure 25 shows demographic trends for workers in the United States, with a declining share of workers in the 16- to 34-year-old age group and a rising share of older workers. Aging of the work force with higher wage scales favors automation, "lean manufacturing," and outsourcing. Figure 25 shows also the trends in average manufacturing wages for the United States, where wages have increased, and for various other countries. In Mainland China, as happened in the United States a century ago, millions of new workers are entering the industrial

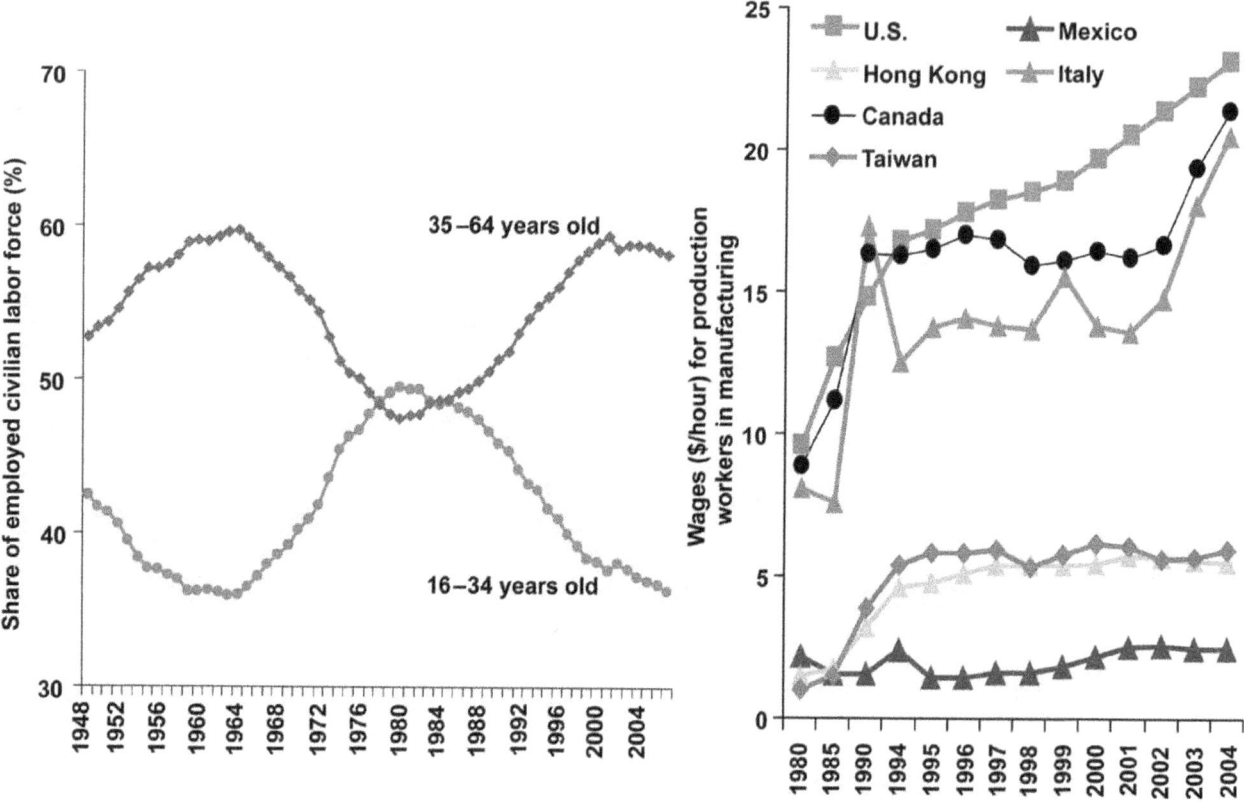

Figure 25—United States demographic trends and manufacturing wage rates in the United States and various other countries: U.S. wages outstrip competitors, a structural phenomenon. Left graph, (Census Bureau 2006b; Economagic 2006); right graph, (Department of Labor 2006).

labor force from the agricultural sector. Wage data for Mainland China are not readily available, but recent manufacturing wages in northern China were reportedly around 60¢ per hour, much lower than in Mexico (Chinafacturing 2006). Furthermore, at current levels of wages and wage appreciation in China, it will take many decades for Chinese wages to approach U.S. wage rates (Banister 2005). One drawback to production in such countries is that there is relatively less to gain from productivity-enhancing technological improvements when wages or are so low. For example, a labor productivity gain of 50% in China would likely provide less economic benefit to furniture producers than a productivity gain of just 10% in the United States. Thus, cheap labor affords less economic incentive for technological innovation. Nevertheless, many new plants in China are operating with modern equipment.

Other reasons besides labor costs are cited for displacement of growth in domestic wood furniture production by imports, such as the following: (1) trade liberalization, which has generally removed previous trade barriers and thereby exposed "vulnerable industries;" (2) readily available global technology that has allowed new competitors with sufficient capital (often with local government support) to combine the best technology with cheap labor to make them "globally competitive," often in a very short period of time;

(3) an uneven "playing field" because environmental and labor regulations in the United States are considered more strict, and such regulations may be lacking in competitor countries; and (4) often currency exchange rates are not favorable, or they are controlled. China, for example, pegged the dollar exchange value of its currency for many years at a low fixed rate of 12.1¢ per yuan (8.277 yuan per dollar), even though the real value of the yuan in China was reportedly higher than the official fixed exchange rate, as indicated by purchasing power parity (CIA 2006). Other factors are often cited, including the corporate tax structure of the United States, the burden of U.S. employee health benefits, or other factors. However, among various factors, extreme discrepancies between wage rates in the United States and competing low-income countries along with imbalances in currency exchange rates stand out in particular as leading elements.

An appropriate question, discussed further below is, What strategic approaches or government policies or programs could really help ameliorate the situation for U.S. furniture producers? In that regard, policies seeking free currency exchange apparently could have significant effects, possibly offsetting competitive advantages of low wage rates. In addition, the world is constantly changing, and manufacturing industries must continuously invest to remain competitive.

Table 1—CAPEX/shipment ratios and trade balances by industry (2000 basis)

Industry	CAPEX/ shipments (%)	Trade balance (billion $)
Wood household furniture	2.1%	– 7
Solid wood products	<1.0%	– 10
Synthetic rubber	6.5%	+ 0.3
Plastics and resins	6.5%	+ 6.2
Automotive parts	5.0%	+ 1
Commercial printing	4.4%	+ 0.4
Agricultural chemicals	4.6%	+ 0.4
Industrial chemicals	8.4%	+ 1
Telephone equipment	3.3%	+ 3
Aircraft parts	5.2%	+ 10

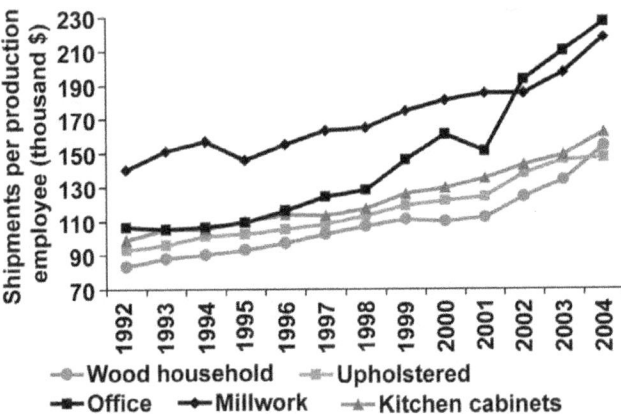

Figure 26—Productivity gains are indicated by trends in shipments per employee in various segments of the U.S. furniture sector (ASM 2006; Census Bureau 2002a).

The U.S. furniture industry appears to be lagging other industries in this regard. As shown in Table 1, industries that spend more on capital expenditures (CAPEX) relative to shipments (CAPEX/shipments) generally have had more favorable trade balances than the furniture industry or other wood products. Any strategy or policy aimed at restoring competitiveness to the U.S. furniture and related industries can be viewed as successful only to the extent that it restores real attractiveness to capital investment in those industries in the United States.

The need for continuous capital investment in the U.S. furniture industry is attenuated by labor productivity improvements in the industry since the early 1990s. Figure 26 illustrates labor productivity improvement in terms of the value of shipments per worker in various segments of the U.S. furniture industry. Output per employee was gradually increasing as the industry entered the recent period of intensified import competition, but the data suggest that a response to import competition has been automation and labor downsizing to achieve more rapid gains in

productivity. Increased productivity no doubt contributed to survival of those U.S. enterprises that became more productive. Productivity gains for furniture producers have begun to rival the productivity gains for other more capital-intensive wood product sectors, such as the pulp and paper sector (where average annual output of paper and paperboard in tons of output per mill employee increased by nearly 70% from 1992 to 2003).

What are the implications for the "supply chain" of wood raw material? Disruptive effects of globalization in furniture and related industries extend far down along raw material supply chains, particularly the supply chain for hardwood lumber. For example, hardwood lumber and veneer produced for furniture have been complementary to hardwood lumber produced for wood pallets, and thus the decline in furniture output affected raw material supply for pallets. The U.S. furniture and veneer industry uses higher grade hardwood logs and lumber while the pallet industry uses lower grade logs and lumber. The higher and lower grades are complementary forest outputs, because logging operations and sawmills produce a mix of higher and lower grade material, as determined primarily by the natural grade distribution of wood in trees harvested from the forest. Thus, as demand for higher grade material waned with declining furniture output, sawmills produced less low-grade material such as pallet stock lumber (a less economical byproduct). Exacerbating the phenomenon of reduced supply for the pallet industry was increased demand for lower grade lumber in the flooring industry, which followed European trends with increased use of lower grade hardwoods in flooring and as output of wood flooring increased in recent years. The supply chain at present also favors flooring over the pallet industry (because of higher product margins).

Figure 27 shows the long-term history of U.S. hardwood lumber production since the late 1800s, along with some recent data on hardwood lumber consumption in the United States during the recent peak production year of 2000 and during a more recent year, 2003. Production history shows an increase in production in recent decades, from around 1980 to the early 1990s, with production peaking in 2000, followed by a decline in production through 2003, mainly associated with the decline in the furniture industry and also wood pallets.

Prior to the big decline in production since 2000, the period from the 1980s to 1990s was an era of "heavy cutting" (Fig. 27), and some might argue that the decline in cutting has a "silver lining," a "good news, bad news story" for forests, inasmuch as the pressure of increasing hardwood timber harvest was reduced. During the 1980s to 1990s period of peak hardwood lumber output, hardwood forests in the eastern United States were often "high-graded" (logged primarily for higher grade hardwood lumber, for export and for domestic furniture production). The effect

25

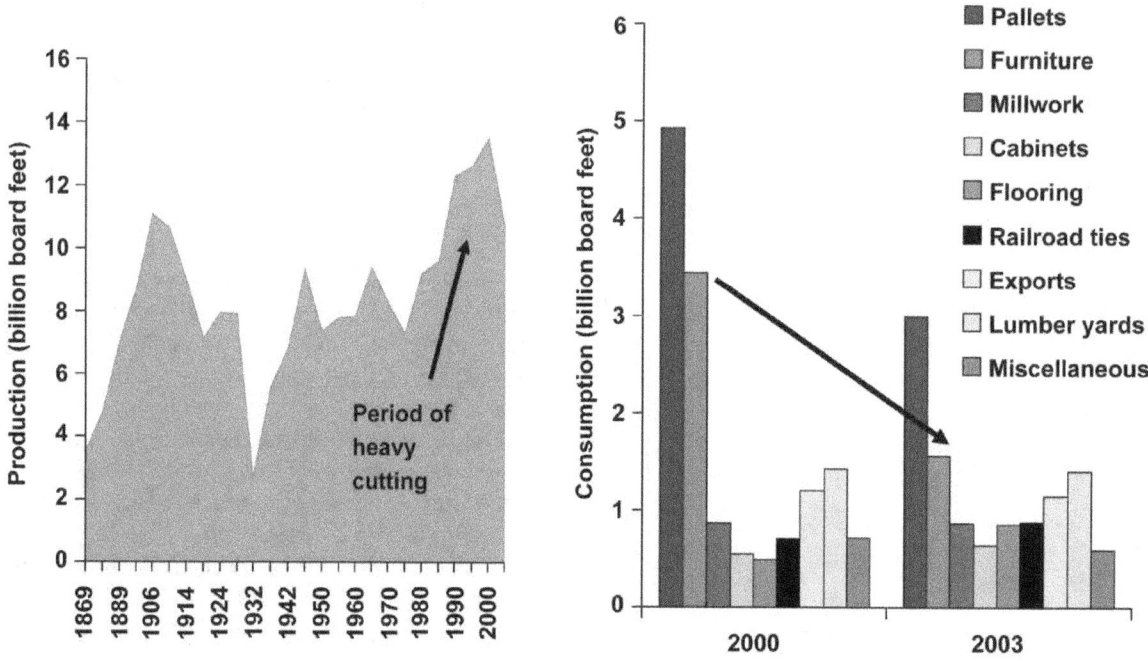

Figure 27—United States annual hardwood lumber production since the 1800s and consumption by end use in 2000 and 2003. Left graph, (Luppold 2006); right graph, (Census Bureau 2002b).

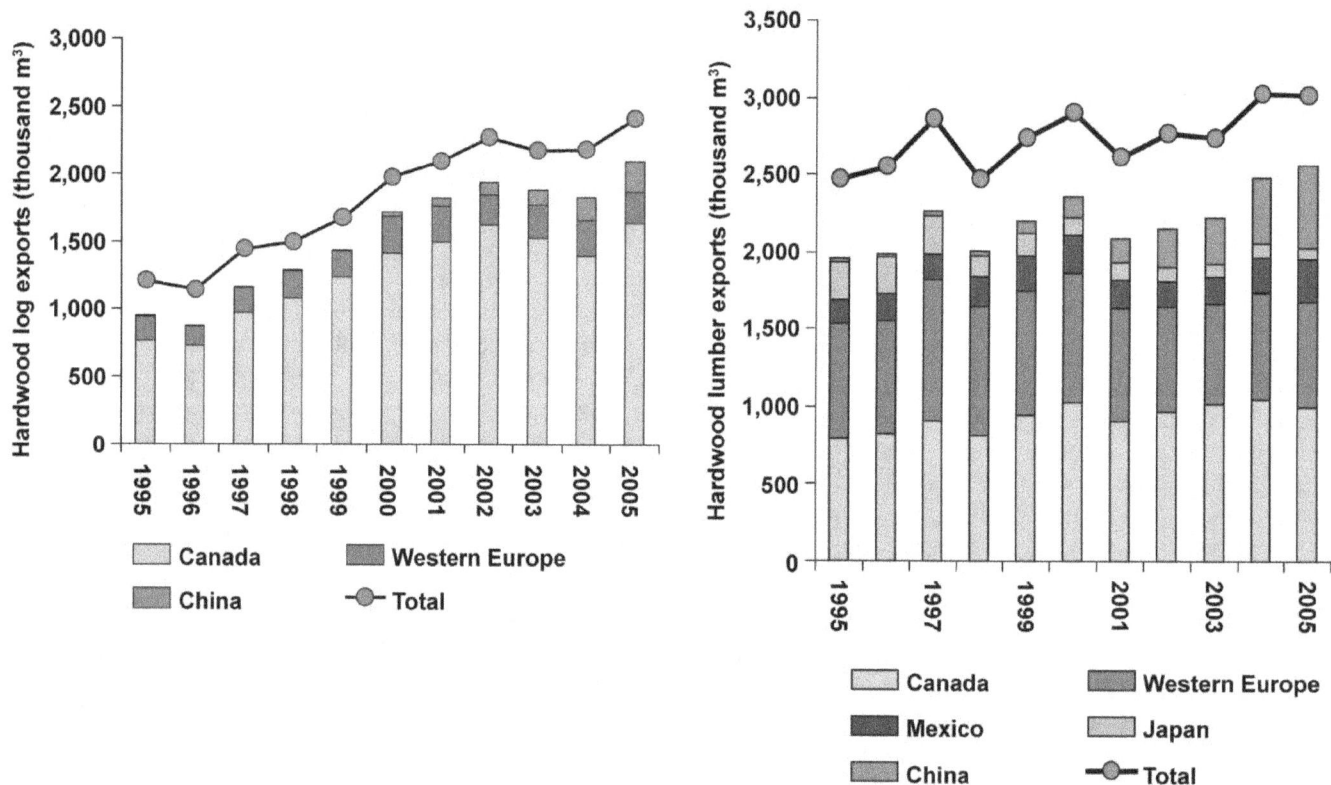

Figure 28—United States hardwood exports, logs and lumber. Competitors buy U.S. logs and lumber to make furniture and export the furniture back to the United States (FAO 2006).

was to leave lower grade standing timber in the forest. High grading tends also to have subtle deleterious effects on stand quality, such as increasing epicormic branching on low-vigor residual trees leading to pin knots (which appear as defects in lumber), or potential genetic regression by leaving inferior stems. Supply chain effects of reduced U.S. demand for hardwood lumber in furniture involved shifts in the grade distribution and value distribution of hardwood lumber and timber output in the United States.

As the value of U.S. furniture industry output declined in recent years, demand for higher grade hardwood logs declined, making the harvest of lower grade hardwood logs less economical. Output declined for lower grades of timber (lower grade logs) that were traditionally co-products in high grading logging operations. An end result was that prices for lower grade hardwood logs and lumber were pushed up because of supply chain disruptions, reducing the use of wood in products made from lower grade lumber such as wooden pallets (Fig. 27). Fortunately, the U.S. pallet industry was able to increase the recycling and re-use of wood pallets, which has to some extent offset the disruptive supply chain effects of globalization in the furniture sector.

The issues of the pallet sector might seem to be minor in the scope of the overall U.S. economy, but wood pallets are used to ship many manufactured commodities in global markets, and standards for wood pallets in international commerce have changed. European standards related to pallets were recently adopted, for example, which complicated shipment to Europe of U.S. goods on pallets that are recycled or re-used (due to contamination issues). Alternatives for the pallet industry besides recycling or re-use include use of more expensive plastic shipping materials or use of softwood lumber instead of low-grade hardwood, thus affecting U.S. export costs more broadly.

As furniture production increased abroad, U.S. hardwood log exports increased—particularly log exports to Canada, as shown in Figure 28. Some of the hardwood log exports were converted into furniture and exported back to the United States. However, export demand was limited for higher grade hardwood lumber in recent years, as global lumber supply competition increased and U.S. hardwood lumber exports shifted toward lower grade lumber, with lower value. As shown in Figure 28, hardwood lumber exports decreased to Western Europe, the region that traditionally purchased higher grade and higher value hardwood lumber stock, while at the same time exports expanded to countries like Canada, China, and Mexico, which imported a lower grade mix of hardwood lumber (with lower value). Hardwood lumber trade with Canada is complex, and U.S.–Canada trade volumes are large, but the volume of hardwood lumber exported from Canada to the United States also increased in recent years. The United States remains a net exporter of hardwood logs and lumber to Canada, but some of the logs exported to Canada are processed into lumber and some are

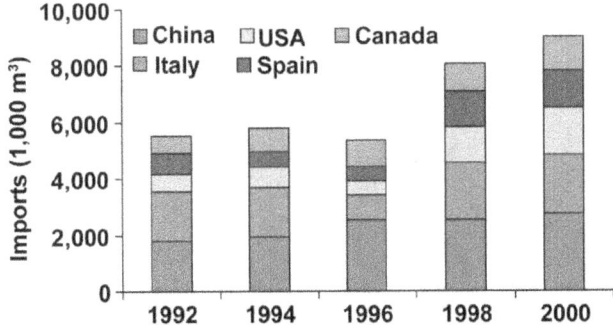

Figure 29—Hardwood lumber imports of top five global hardwood importers (Taylor 2002).

shipped back to the United States, while some are also exported elsewhere from Canada or used to produce furniture or pallets in Canada.

Furthermore, other competing global sources of hardwood lumber exist, so the United States faces competition in exporting hardwood lumber to global markets. In 2000, for example, the world as a whole imported approximately 10 million m^3 of hardwood lumber, 7 million of which came from sources other than the United States—chiefly Eastern Europe, Southeast Asia, South America, and Russia. Thus, even if the U.S. furniture industry continues to recede and capacity growth moves abroad as it has in recent years, it is by no means certain that the demand for U.S. hardwood logs and lumber in the furniture industry will be replaced by log or lumber export demand. China has emerged in recent years as the leading global hardwood lumber importer, followed by Italy, as shown in the chart of imports for the top five hardwood lumber importers (Fig. 29). The top importers of hardwood lumber are also among the top exporters of furniture to the United States, but only a small fraction of their imports of hardwood lumber come from the United States.

In summary, the balance between demand for lower and higher grade hardwood lumber has shifted with reduced demand for higher grade lumber in the furniture industry and for export. This shift in demand has had a distinct effect on the supply chain for other hardwood products such as pallets. Since furniture and wood pallets are by far the largest markets for hardwood lumber (Fig. 27), they largely drive the U.S. hardwood lumber market. In particular, economic returns in hardwood forest management are driven by trends in the furniture industry, as it represents the largest demand for higher grade lumber and higher grade logs. The shift in value of hardwood log and lumber output has affected revenues to hardwood sawmills, logging contractors, and the forestry sector in general, particularly managers of largely private eastern hardwood forests. Historically, higher grade logs provided the bulk of timber revenues for hardwood forest landowners and paid most of the bills for loggers of hardwood timber. If landowners find it less profitable to sell hardwood timber, they may be more inclined sell their

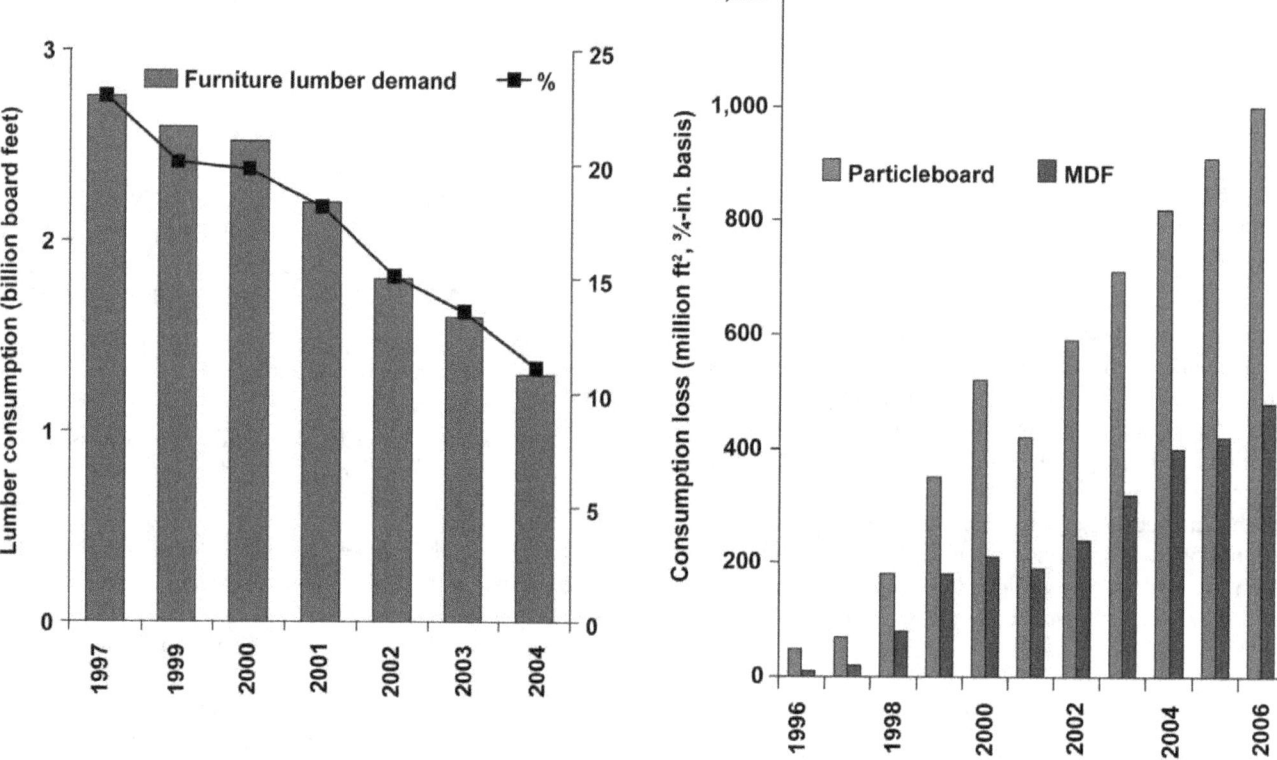

Figure 30—Supply chain effects: the "domino effects" of declining furniture output on hardwood lumber, particleboard, and medium density fiberboard (MDF). Sources: left graph, hardwood lumber purchased by U.S. furniture manufacturers in decline (Hardwood Market Report 2005), right graph, loss of North American MDF and particleboard demand due to furniture imports (RISI 2003).

land for other higher value purposes such as housing development.

Finally, declining furniture output affects raw material supply chains other than hardwood lumber, including particleboard, MDF, and veneer industries. Figure 30 illustrates "domino effects" of declining furniture output in terms of declining purchases of hardwood lumber by furniture manufacturers and losses of particleboard and MDF demand due to furniture imports. Meanwhile China became the world's leading producer of MDF in 2003, after experiencing a 20-fold increase in capacity over the preceding decade, and continued growth of MDF in China is expected along with expanding furniture output (RISI 2003).

Are effective policy responses to these phenomena likely? And, if so, what are likely implications for sustainable forestry? There are as many potential responses to these phenomena as there are recognized causes, but not every response may be implemented or effective. Among the recognized causes are trade liberalization, global access to advanced technology, significant differentials in wage rates between furniture producers in the United States and low-wage competing countries like China, differentials between the United States and other countries in environmental standards and labor regulations or compliance, regulation of currency exchange rates such as China's fixing of

the U.S. dollar/Chinese yuan exchange rate in recent years, differentials in health and safety benefits for employees, differentials in the structure of corporate tax rates, and differentials in capital investment, technological development, and infrastructure. It is difficult to envision that internal strategies of the U.S. furniture industry or hardwood lumber sector alone will be effective responses, because the causes extend beyond the hardwood sector or may be otherwise intractable.

For example, given the demographic distribution of the aging U.S. labor force (Fig. 25) and relatively high standards of living in the United States, it is fairly impractical to envision that furniture industry competitiveness could be restored by drastically reducing wage rates or health and safety benefits for U.S. furniture workers. This scenario is particularly unlikely to result from an internal government policy or industrial strategy. Indeed, wage rates in the U.S. manufacturing sector have increased in recent years (Fig. 25), partly because increased automation and other technological advances required an increasingly skilled workforce. Although downsizing, outsourcing, and "off shoring" of furniture production have been rampant in recent years, there has been no movement toward drastically reducing wages at U.S. furniture plants as a means of restoring competitiveness. Thus, employment in U.S.

non-upholstered wood household furniture production dropped by about one-third from 1999 to 2004, but average hourly earnings of production workers within that sector increased by about 15% in the same period (BLS 2005).

Similarly, wholesale abandonment of free trade, labor regulations, or environmental policies or sweeping changes in corporate tax structure are neither likely, nor can they be expected to result immediately from U.S. government policies or industrial strategies. In the long run, however, policies might shift to some extent in recognition of the need to support competitiveness of U.S. industry. That leaves for consideration the matters of fixed currency exchange rates, capital investment, and development of technology and infrastructure as open avenues for government policy or industrial strategy in seeking to overcome current competitiveness challenges faced by the U.S. furniture industry.

Along those avenues, solving the matter of fixed or artificially low currency exchange rates in low income countries would appear to offer significant potential benefits for U.S. furniture manufacturers. As indicated previously, furniture producers in Mainland China are estimated to have roughly a 30% cost advantage over producers in the United States, owing primarily to extremely low wage rates in China. China is also the leading exporter of wood household furniture to the United States, and China for years pegged its currency at a low fixed exchange rate with the U.S. dollar (12.1¢ per yuan) a value well below the real purchasing power parity of the currency in China. This circumstance offset the leading economic rationale for free trade, by keeping dollar-denominated wages so low in China that Chinese workers could not purchase U.S. goods in exchange for their labor. Nevertheless, China attracted investment in manufacturing of goods for shipment to the United States. Estimates by economists have suggested that a free currency exchange could result in the dollar exchange rate in China rising by 15% to 25% (Lardy 2003). According to Nicholas R. Lardy, Senior Fellow, Institute for International Economics, Washington, D.C., in testimony before the House of Representatives Committee on International Relations, October 21, 2003, estimates of under valuation range from 10% to 40%, but a range from 15% to 25% appears most likely. This would logically result in a similar increase in the cost of furniture made in China and sold in the United States, reducing the cost advantage of furniture production in China. Many countries besides China engage in currency intervention of one sort or the other, and U.S. furniture producers would likely benefit from less intervention and a more generally accepted free exchange of currencies in the global market. Achieving that outcome would entail working diplomatically with other countries and also through the currency exchange policies of the International Monetary Fund (IMF), which govern the latitude for currency intervention by individual countries.

Beyond seeking free currency exchange, strategic approaches that may help restore U.S. furniture industry competitiveness include those that promote capital investment, technological development, or infrastructure development in the furniture sector, including investment in forestry to provide hardwood timber resources for furniture and related industries. One such approach is product certification. Product certification has become more common in marketing of hardwood forest products in the United States and abroad, with an increasing but still modest success in expanding the demand for products that are certified to derive from forests managed under sustainable guidelines. Most hardwood logs and lumber produced in the United States are harvested from naturally regenerated forests that are usually managed on a sustainable basis, so it may be possible for U.S. manufacturers of hardwood furniture and related products to obtain wider environmental certification of their products as a marketing strategy.

Another strategic approach gaining recognition in the hardwood processing industry is a shift in the business paradigm focused on restructuring, domestically and internationally. Automation, lean manufacturing, and global enterprise development are part of this approach, including expanded use of imported components, subassemblies, along with "just in time" manufacturing methods and improved supply chain management. The end result may be a larger and more global secondary processing industry (with expanded global trade in wood furniture components), and perhaps a smaller primary industry in the United States (lumber and dimension stock). With the advance of the Internet or electronic commerce, this business paradigm shift will encompass the way that furniture is designed, customized, marketed, and distributed in the future.

In general, what are the likely implications for sustainable forest management of alternative policies or industrial strategies aimed at coping with globalization, consolidation, and structural change in the furniture sector? As suggested above, international currency policies that effectively replace fixed exchange rates with free exchange of currencies could go a long way toward erasing artificial cost advantages in furniture production in some low-income countries where fixed exchange rates have kept dollar-denominated wages and costs artificially low. By placing U.S. furniture manufacturers on a more level playing field, elimination of fixed exchange rates would help restore competitiveness and growth to the U.S. industry, and by extension help recover some of the recently lost value and output of the U.S. hardwood lumber and related sectors. A similar but somewhat less certain outcome might be obtained by wider adoption of sustainable forest product certification in the U.S. furniture industry. However, thus far U.S. wood product customers appear to show limited recognition or differentiation of value in forest products produced under sustainable forest management guidelines. At least many customers do not appear generally willing to pay large price premiums for environmentally certified products (many customers tend to shop instead for design and functionality at a bargain price regardless of where the product or wood raw materials may have originated).

Finally, the strategies of automation, restructuring, and lean manufacturing, with implicit requirements for more capital-intensive enterprise development, will no doubt continue to be pursued by many surviving firms in the U.S. furniture, hardwood component, and hardwood lumber industries. However, it is dubious whether increasing scale of production or productivity through automation or lean manufacturing can alone compensate for cost advantages of producers in low-wage countries because of huge wage differentials plus global access to advanced technology. Skilled and productive American workers have demonstrated an ability to keep many steps ahead of workers in other countries in terms of productivity, but still U.S. labor costs in furniture production are much higher than in low-wage countries, and it is difficult to imagine that gains in worker productivity alone could outpace the enormous differentials in wage rates. This is particularly true for furniture, given the labor-intensive nature of furniture production and that workers in competing countries also increasingly have access to advanced production facilities and technology. This is not, however, to suggest that strategies of automation, lean manufacturing, and capital-intensive enterprise development are inappropriate to the furniture industry. Indeed, the general response of U.S. industry to import competition has been to shift toward more capital- and skill-intensive enterprises. We simply suggest that those strategies may need to be augmented by other strategies. Improved productivity will be necessary to compete but alone may not be sufficient.

One thing that appears fairly clear is that successful U.S. furniture manufacturers are becoming increasingly nimble, more globally connected, and better able to respond quickly to global opportunities. Today's furniture consumers want product uniqueness at a competitive price, and as with kitchen cabinet customers, they want good quality furniture that is different than their neighbor's furniture. Thus, efficient product customization has been recognized as a key to competitiveness in the furniture sector, rather than just "mass production." Traditionally, proximity to the customers afforded local producers an ability to know better the customer needs and to more efficiently provide customized furniture products for those needs. Today, however, global communication networks and global enterprise development allow instantaneous communication of information such as custom product specifications around the globe. Already in the U.S. furniture industry, global enterprise development is taking place, with U.S. furniture producers shifting their production or component procurement operations from the local or regional scale to the international scale, facilitated by global communication networks, and often achieving

significant cost savings or more efficient product development as a beneficial result.

As in the past, the hardwood product industries will continue to produce and sell products valued and differentiated by consumers largely on the basis of appearance and functionality. These will include furniture, millwork, cabinetry, and flooring, as well as hardwood lumber, plywood, and the products of veneer mills that supply material to those industries, along with the logging industries that supply logs to mills. There are at the extreme two broad business strategies that producers of end products in this sector can choose: (1) competition based on cost and price leadership, with mass production and economies of scale yielding economic value or (2) market differentiation with customer service and product value yielding economic value. The reality is that successful furniture producers, either in the United States or abroad, pursue an optimal combination of these strategies, using the best of both.

Producers of furniture and furniture components in countries like China are emerging with a fairly clear advantage on the basis of cost and price leadership, primarily due to extremely low wage rates and partly due to artificially low exchange rates, but they are also learning how to compete on the basis of product quality, appearance, and design. United States manufacturers may seem to have an advantage in product differentiation because of proximity to the large U.S. market and better understanding of the U.S. consumer, but global enterprise development and efficient global business connections actually give foreign business partners rapid access to information about U.S. customer needs and product specifications.

Thus, one more significant structural change associated with economic globalization is the emergence of global enterprise development, with enhanced capability for global interconnectedness in product design, production, and marketing technology. Modern computer systems and information technologies facilitate increasingly swift and nimble business transactions across international borders, allowing firms at all levels of the supply chain and in various countries to operate together in the fluid and constantly changing global market environment. As shown by the capability of foreign furniture producers to penetrate deeply into U.S. wood furniture markets in recent years, global enterprises are learning how to respond as efficiently and rapidly as local firms to the needs and whims of furniture consumers, both in the United States and abroad.

Will these structural changes mean increased or decreased demand for U.S. hardwood lumber? Thus far, the evidence suggests reduced domestic demand for hardwood lumber and reduced demand for export, with some increase in demand for hardwood log export but not enough to compensate for reduced lumber demand. It also appears to be resulting in a shift toward reduced demand for higher grade (and higher value) hardwood lumber, with resulting implications for hardwood forest management—perhaps less high grading in general, but also less revenues for loggers and forestry operations with less higher grade or higher value log output. In the absence of significant change, the U.S. furniture industry may continue to shrink, with consequences for the entire hardwood lumber and related industries. Unless the decline of the U.S. furniture industry can be reversed, implications for forest management include much less certainty about maintaining or enhancing the multiple socioeconomic benefits that could be associated with sustainable management of hardwood timber resources in the United States.

Softwood Lumber and Housing

Softwood Sawmills

"Softwood" refers to coniferous species of trees, such as pine, fir, and spruce. United States pulp mills consume a larger quantity of wood than U.S. softwood sawmills, if wood residues are included, but softwood sawmills consume a larger quantity of roundwood timber. Softwood sawmills produce softwood lumber, the largest consumer of industrial roundwood and largest single category of solid wood products produced in the United States. Structural change in the U.S. softwood lumber industry is a long-run historical process, operating under competitive pressures to reduce production costs and timber costs. Globalization widened the scope of that process. Until the mid-20th century, the process was largely confined within U.S. borders. In early U.S. history, production was centered in the Northeast where many small sawmills operated on a localized basis. With the advent of railroads and decreasing transportation costs in the mid 1800s, the softwood lumber industry shifted into the Great Lake States. Sawmills also became much larger and were able to serve wider markets. Around 1900, as the Great Lake States resource began to wane, softwood lumber production moved to the West and South, reaching an apex in the West around the mid 1950s but continuing to expand in the South.

Since timber costs are the largest share of softwood lumber production costs, timber availability and expense was a primary historical driver of regional shifts in the softwood lumber industry. Thus, as the softwood timber resource was depleted in one region, the industry gravitated to other regions with cheaper and more abundant timber. A significant shift in North American softwood lumber production occurred with the easing of tariff barriers following World War II, enabling low-cost Canadian lumber producers to gain greater access to U.S. markets. As a result, the pendulum swung away from the U.S. West in favor primarily of Canada, and secondarily the U.S. South (Fig. 31).

Import quotas on softwood lumber from Canada in the 1990s and more recent U.S. countervailing and antidumping duties of up to 29% limited the growth of Canada's market

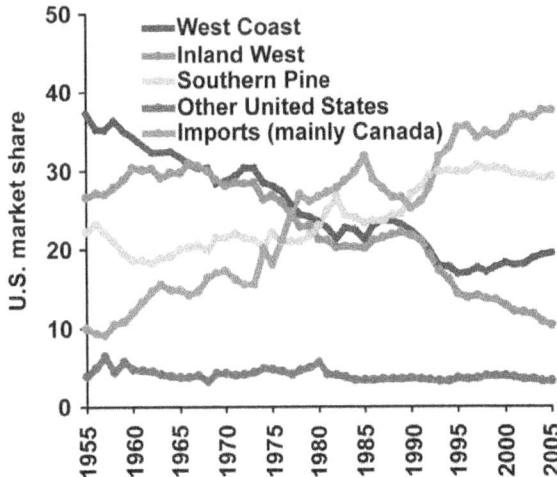

Figure 31—Evolution of U.S. softwood lumber market shares by source, 1955–2005 (WWPA 2004; U.S. Department of Commerce 2005).

share over the past decade. Remarkably, however, Canadian lumber producers still maintained one-third share in the U.S. softwood lumber market by 2005. The ability of Canadian lumber producers to maintain a strong market share despite import duties may be attributable to a strategy of closing less efficient sawmills and upgrading larger facilities with newer and more efficient equipment. An article by Gordon Hamilton in the Vancouver Sun newspaper, May 1, 2004, reported that conversion costs for the Canadian lumber corporation Canfor dropped by 30% since 1998 (Hamilton 2004). Earlier in the year, Canfor completed a $26 million (Canadian dollars) upgrade to its Houston, British Columbia, dimension lumber mill, reportedly reducing unit costs there by 24%, and making it the world's largest softwood lumber mill, with an output capacity of 600 million board feet per year (Tice 2004). The output capacity of that one Canfor mill is roughly 10 times greater than the average output capacity of U.S. softwood sawmills. Meanwhile, as shown in Figure 32, the average output capacity of U.S. mills has increased and number of mills has declined, as smaller and less efficient sawmills were closed.

Additionally, global trade liberalization and further reductions in transportation costs provided opportunities for new suppliers from other areas of the globe. Though small individually, softwood lumber suppliers in Chile, New Zealand, Brazil, Mexico, and Europe collectively achieved significant U.S. market penetration (Fig. 33). Imports from non-Canadian sources expanded with reduced barriers to cross-border trade, as imports from Canada were hampered by quotas and tariffs. From the mid-1990s onward, a strong U.S. dollar encouraged higher imports in general, including imports from non-Canadian sources. In 2003 higher ocean freight rates and a lower U.S. dollar value briefly stanched the flow of imports from non-Canadian sources, but the flow increased again with a higher Canadian dollar since 2003. By 2005, softwood lumber imports from non-Canadian

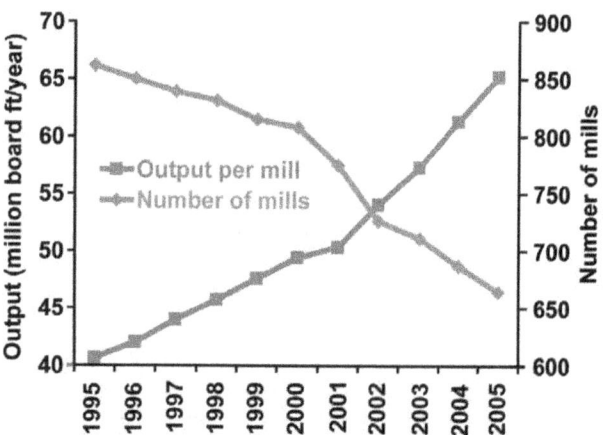

Figure 32—Total number of major U.S. softwood sawmills and average output capacity per mill, 1995–2005 (Spelter and Alderman 2003).

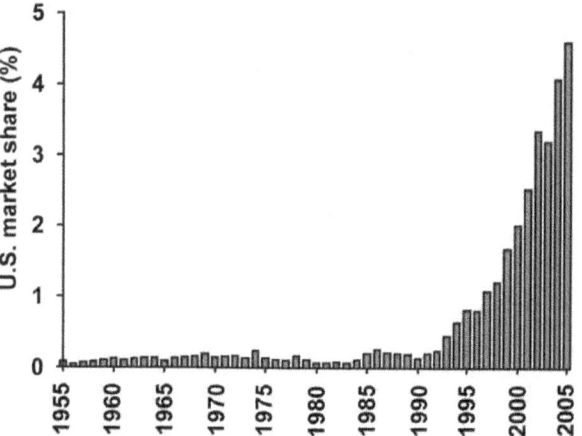

Figure 33—Evolution of non-Canadian market share in U.S. softwood lumber market, 1955–2005 (U.S. Department of Commerce 2005).

sources reached levels more than 10 times higher than in the early 1990s.

The influx of softwood lumber from non-Canadian sources reflects also another significant structural change in U.S. lumber markets that is not apparent from the percentage of total consumption alone. The structural change has involved displacement of U.S. market share in the highest grades and more expensive categories of softwood lumber. Softwood lumber is sold in a variety of standard grades, and imports actually displaced a much higher proportion of U.S. market share for wood molding and the so-called "clear" grades (knot-free or low-defect grades) used for millwork, such as "shop and better" grade.

As recently as 1990, U.S. producers accounted for nearly 90% of U.S. consumption of shop and better grade softwood lumber, with total consumption at around 3 billion board feet (Wood Markets 2004). Such lumber was traditionally produced in the United States primarily from larger

or old-growth ponderosa pine trees and other western U.S. tree species, but U.S. supplies of such timber have been declining since the late 1980s. By 2003, consumption of shop and better grade lumber had dropped to about half of its 1990 level, as U.S. output receded and as molded fiberboard and other materials increasingly displaced lumber in molding and millwork. Meanwhile, U.S. imports of wood for shop and better grade lumber more than tripled during that period. By 2003 imported wood accounted for more than 60% of shop and better grade lumber consumption in the United States (Wood Markets 2004). The bulk of those imports consisted of wood from plantation-grown pine trees that were specifically cultivated and pruned to produce clear lumber, in countries such as Chile, Brazil, and New Zealand. The competitive influx of clear wood imports from overseas plantations contributed to the decline of clear lumber produced from domestic timber, the output of which had dropped by 2003 to only about one-quarter of its 1990 level.

United States imports of wood molding products also increased substantially, with roughly a four-fold increase in the period from 1990 to 2003 (FAS 2003). United States solid-wood molding products accounted for roughly three-fourths of U.S. consumption in 1990, but that market share was steadily eroded since then. United States solid-wood molding producers had only about a one-third share of the U.S. molding market by 2003, displaced largely by imported solid-wood molding (chiefly from Chile and Brazil) and also by molding material made from MDF (Wood Markets 2004).

Thus, since 1990 economic globalization contributed to structural changes in the sourcing of clear grade softwood lumber and molding, as domestic species (e.g., ponderosa pine) were largely replaced in the market by imports and other materials. Structural changes included declining availability of ponderosa pine, expanded output of clear wood from highly productive overseas plantations, and expanded use of lower cost MDF in place of solid-wood material. Collectively, these changes deeply affected the U.S. market for higher valued softwood lumber products. The net effect in terms of forestry revenues was a notable decline in output of higher grade logs and higher value timber that were once used in much larger volumes to produce clear lumber grades and solid-wood molding products. There was also a notable loss in revenues for softwood lumber producers because of the decline in output of clear grades of softwood lumber and solid-wood molding.

The intensity of international competition in softwood lumber and building materials contributed to gradual attrition of U.S. softwood sawmills, as growing demand created a competitive drive toward efficiency and economies of scale among survivors. As shown in Figure 32, the number of major U.S. softwood sawmills dropped by 23% from 862 in 1995 to 664 in 2005, but there was a 60% increase in average capacity of U.S. softwood sawmills. Consolidation, cost-saving technology, and larger scale were the principal means within control of the industry to stay globally competitive. Another policy lever, but on a national scale beyond industry control, is policies related to currency exchange rates, the movement of which can offset or reinforce cost control measures or technological improvement autonomously undertaken by suppliers.

Dynamics of global trade and increased foreign and domestic competition also spurred corporate consolidation, although the U.S. softwood lumber industry remains a highly fragmented industry. The top 20 U.S. firms, for example, accounted for only about 55% of total industry output in 2003 (Table 2).

Striving for competitive economies of scale and production efficiency via consolidation and structural change are universal drivers of economic globalization, yet certain niche opportunities for small-scale sawmills may continue to exist in some cases. One such case may be found in the U.S. West, where reduced and variable supplies of timber originate from public lands. In that region, small-scale (almost portable) sawmills are emerging, geared to processing timber from forest thinning operations on public lands. In some cases small-scale operators produce rough-sawn lumber and ship it to larger facilities for finishing. These "micro mills," sometimes operating on a part-time or intermittent basis, represent a response to the uncertainties and variability inherent in public timber supply, which is often subject to legal challenges or harvest constraints.

By keeping the size of operation small, capital investment and financial risks are reduced. Small investment and small scale can also afford intermittent operation, swinging into production when wood supply is available and lumber prices are favorable, but shutting down when not. The semi-portability feature also adds assurance that if timber supply in one region is cut off, equipment is transportable to another site where timber is available. Also, a small-scale operation may have less likelihood of public objections to forest thinning operations on public lands (mainly aimed at reducing fire hazards). Thus, in these special circumstances, reduced financial risks and small scale of operation may afford a niche opportunity for small sawmills, but such mills still face real challenges competing on the basis of costs, productivity, and profitability against increasingly larger and more automated mills elsewhere. Small-scale micromills account for only a small fraction of softwood lumber output nationwide (perhaps 2% or less). Furthermore, the demand for efficiency has resulted in some big and highly automated small-log mills (taking advantage of low wood input costs with cheaper small logs), and such mills can shift demand from larger logs to smaller logs. In some local areas, larger logs are being discounted in price because of difficulty in finding buyers for larger logs (Erb 2001).

Table 2—Top 20 U.S. softwood lumber producers in 2003[a]

Company	No. mills	Production	Cumulative
Weyerhaeuser	29	4,884	4,884
International Paper	21	2,200	7,084
Georgia Pacific	20	1,730	8,814
Sierra Pacific	14	1,556	10,370
Hampton Affiliates	6	1,294	11,664
Stimson Lumber	10	1,039	12,703
Temple Inland	7	865	13,568
Simpson Timber	5	840	14,408
Potlatch	5	807	15,215
RSG Lumber	6	687	15,902
Louisiana Pacific	6	600	16,502
Gilman Building	6	573	17,075
Swanson	3	437	17,512
Plum Creek	6	406	17,918
New South	3	375	18,293
Pacific Lumber Company	3	365	18,658
Boise Cascade	7	356	19,014
Seneca Sawmills	3	317	19,331
West Fraser Timber	2	299	19,630
Crown Pacific	3	292	19,922

[a]Million board feet, Wood Markets 2004.

Housing

Housing construction in the United States was also affected by economic globalization but in a more roundabout way. Unlike manufacturing, home building is a very localized industry, not as readily subject to the influence of trade, direct outsourcing, or displacement by competitors in low-income countries (although some U.S. construction firms have hired resident aliens or recent immigrants). Thus, the construction industry as a whole did not experience as much direct effect from globalization as manufacturing. Instead, effects of economic globalization on U.S. housing construction came about circuitously in ways that generally benefited housing construction.

In general, expansion of global trade allowed entry for more of the world's population into the global economic arena. Global enterprises have found new masses of workers in low-income countries willing to perform fungible manufacturing tasks at considerably lower wages than in developed countries. This has led to a transfer of jobs to low-income countries, leaving voids of employment within some manufacturing sectors in the developed economies, such as the steel and textile industries of the United States, for example. Rigidities inherent in the displacement of large numbers of workers and the displacement of production capacity have made developed economies less responsive to traditional levers of economic management and fiscal or monetary stimuli.

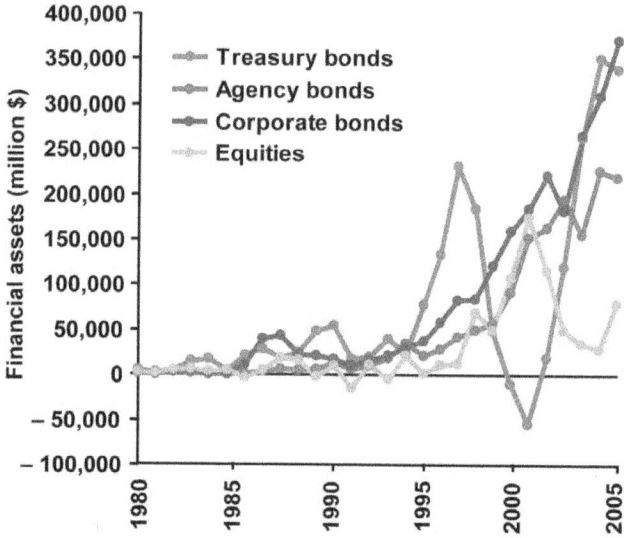

Figure 34—Net foreign purchases of U.S. financial assets, 1980–2005 (U.S. Treasury 2005).

Thus, to achieve a given response in economic activity, government fiscal and monetary policies have needed in recent years to be stronger than in previous "pre-globalization" periods. Significantly more aggressive monetary policies, leading to barely positive interest rates, consequently provided a disproportionate boost to interest-sensitive sectors, the most important of which is home building. Moreover, newly integrated economic regions have striven to maintain favorable terms of trade and have been recycling increasing amounts of their dollar earnings (from trade surpluses) back into the U.S. economy to keep exchange rates competitive. This has taken the form of direct purchases of U.S. financial assets, chiefly U.S. government bonds and increasingly also bonds of U.S. government-sponsored agencies, foremost among which are the various mortgage-lending entities that

supply the bulk of the mortgage funds for U.S. home buying. These purchases have enabled the level of interest rates for home mortgages to stay lower for longer than would have been possible without the infusion of foreign capital.

The expanding scale of foreign intervention is evident in Figure 34, showing the recent influx of foreign funds to purchase U.S. financial assets. In 2005, foreign purchases of corporate bonds exceeded similar purchases of treasury bonds, while purchases of agency bonds were not far behind. Purchases of treasury bonds and notes amounted to $339 billion while corporate bond purchases were $372 billion, purchases of equities were $80 billion, and agency bond purchases amounted to $220 billion. Together these amounted to just over $1 trillion, not far above the $783 billion current account trade deficit. This ongoing infusion of foreign funds has contributed to exceptionally low interest rates, the first-order determinant of robust housing activity in the United States. Foreign purchases of U.S. agency bonds alone (used primarily to fund home mortgage loans) represented a direct infusion of funds to housing amounting to over $100,000 per each new housing unit built in 2005. Thus, softwood sawmills and housing benefited directly from U.S. trade deficits and return flows of investment dollars through the boost given to home construction financing and ultimately home construction.

Given that U.S. home mortgages have come to rely on global financing, it is not surprising to find parallel trends in U.S. housing starts and the U.S. trade deficit. Figure 35 illustrates parallel trends in monthly U.S. housing starts (at an annual rate) and the monthly U.S. trade deficit in goods from 1995 through 2005. As the trade deficit soared to record levels, dollars sent overseas returned in record foreign purchases of agency bonds, used to finance home mortgage loans. Thus, U.S. housing starts have climbed in parallel with the

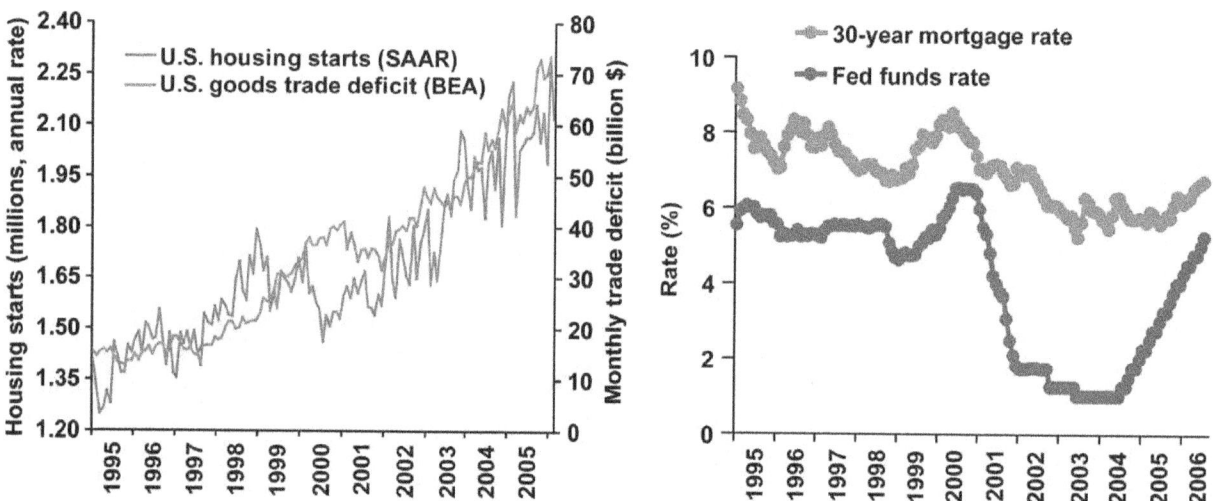

Figure 35—Monthly U.S. housing starts (annual basis) and U.S. trade deficit in goods, 1995–2005, along with trends in average 30-year mortgage and Federal Funds rates (BEA 2004; Federal Reserve 2006b, Freddie Mac 2006). SAAR, seasonally adjusted annual rate.

trade deficit since the mid-1990s. Housing starts leveled out for a period (1999–2000) when the Federal Reserve raised short-term interest rates, causing mortgage rates to rise briefly (Fig. 35), but foreign purchases of U.S. financial assets continued to expand and helped push mortgage rates back down. Expanding liquidity from foreign purchases of financial assets plus a lowering of interest rates by the Federal Reserve provided low-interest financing that stimulated the continued housing boom from 2001 to 2005, when housing starts increased by about 30%. Notably, the most recent housing boom (2001–2005) began at a time when overall U.S. payroll employment was receding (particularly in manufacturing) with slower growth in real employee compensation, and thus the housing boom was driven more by cheap financing than income growth (Bazdarich and Thornberg 2004). The average size of new homes and amount of wood consumed in housing construction also increased in recent years. However, in 2006 rising interest rates and decreasing affordability due to elevated home prices had negative consequences for U.S. housing construction activity.

Wood Panel Sector (OSB, Plywood, Other Wood Panels)

This section discusses several questions related to the wood panel sector: (1) How did the U.S. wood panel sector come under the influence of economic globalization? (2) What are primary determinants of competitive position in wood panels, and how has the U.S. industry responded? (3) What else can be done, if anything, to improve the situation?

Coming Under the Influence of Globalization

Economic globalization directly influenced growth in some parts of the U.S. wood panel sector in recent years, such as the particleboard and MDF industries that experienced weaker product demands for furniture manufacture because of expanded wood furniture imports. For structural wood panels such as plywood and OSB (used for roof, floor, and wall sheathing in building construction), the influence of globalization evolved circuitously from earlier developments in the domestic wood panel industry. Until the early 1980s, softwood plywood was the only commercially significant structural wood panel product made in North America, and up until around 1960 all softwood plywood in the United States was made in the Pacific Northwest (PNW) region, primarily using Douglas-fir peeler logs for veneer. Subsequently, however, growth in structural wood panel output shifted to other regions, other products, and other countries.

In the 1980s, resolution of environmental issues concerning management of old-growth Douglas-fir on public lands in the PNW region began to have notable effects on availability of larger Douglas-fir peeler logs. At that time, the plywood industry in the PNW region tried to increase product recovery in response to increased wood costs, while shifting to the use of lower grade logs for much of their veneer. In

that context, competitive pressures from plywood producers in the U.S. South had big effects on the western plywood industry, as did the later adoption of OSB as a substitute for plywood. Most U.S. softwood plywood was still made in the PNW region up until the 1980s. Softwood plywood based on Southern Pine began to be produced in the early 1960s. In the late 1980s and early 1990s, harvest of Douglas-fir on public lands in the PNW region declined dramatically with shifts in timber management policy, and thus the supply of Douglas-fir timber declined, particularly supply of larger peeler logs used for plywood. Peeler log prices increased because of reduced supply and so did plywood manufacturing costs, at first in the PNW region and then also eventually in the South as softwood plywood production capacity moved from the PNW region to the South and demand for larger logs increased in that region.

The upward shift in plywood production costs favored development of a substitute wood panel product, OSB, made from lower value pulpwood raw material rather than the higher value softwood peeler logs or veneer logs required for softwood plywood. Figure 36 shows the historical decline in timber harvest that occurred in the PNW region during the late 1980s and early 1990s in the leading softwood plywood producing states of Washington and Oregon. Figure 36 shows also corresponding trends in estimated average variable costs of production for softwood plywood in the PNW region and for plywood and OSB in the U.S. South.

Because it costs less than plywood, OSB has clear competitive advantages, particularly for standard commodity grades of sheathing used in housing construction where cost competitiveness is a crucial factor. By 2004, nearly 90% of North American OSB demand was being used in housing construction and remodeling, with the remainder used in industrial uses and non-residential construction (APA 2006c). Thus, OSB production expanded rapidly since the early 1980s, and OSB captured a dominant share of the large North American market for structural wood panels in housing construction. Production costs rose for both OSB and plywood from 2002 to 2005, because of higher costs for energy, adhesives, and wood, but a housing boom during that period ensured continued demand, despite higher prices.

The structural wood panel market was previously dominated by softwood plywood, but as shown in Figure 37, the market share generally expanded for OSB compared with softwood plywood in North America since OSB was introduced commercially around 1980. Furthermore, softwood plywood was made primarily in the United States, but OSB was made increasingly in Canada as well as in the United States. Essentially, OSB technology was both more economical than softwood plywood (Fig. 36) and also more in tune with the evolving wood resource supply situation, capable of using relatively abundant supplies of pulpwood and a more diverse array of hardwood and softwood species, thus

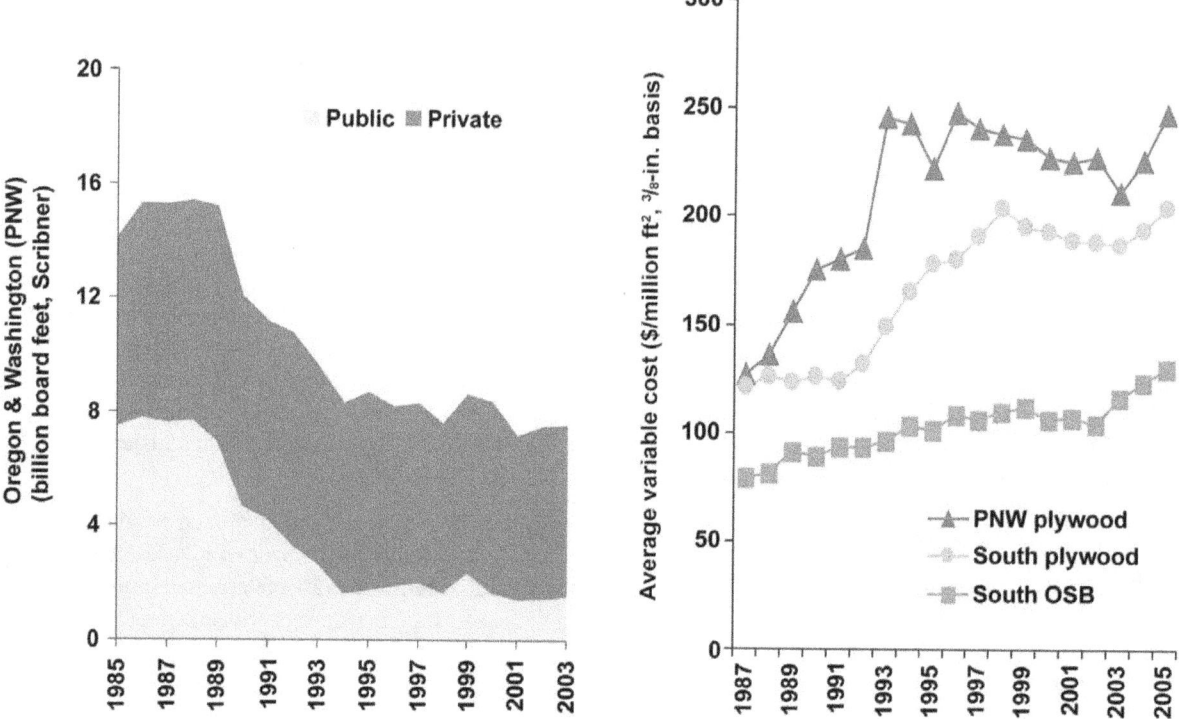

Figure 36—Timber harvest trend for public and private timberland in Washington and Oregon (PNW), and effect on variable costs of production for structural wood panels. Left graph, (Warren 2005); right graph, (RISI 2004a).

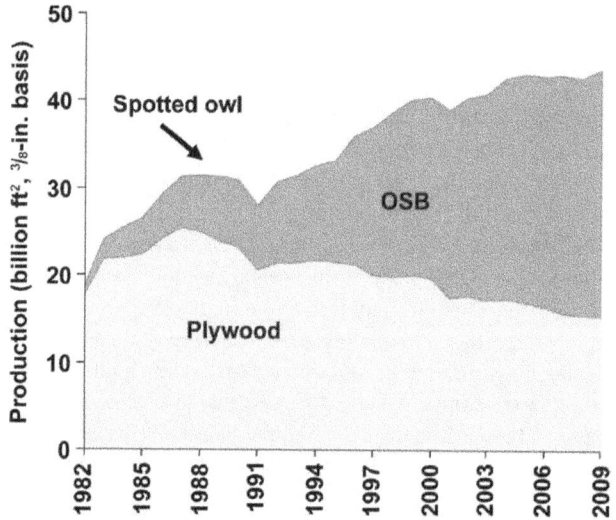

Figure 37—Shifts in North American structural panel market share following resolution of the 1980s spotted owl issue in the Pacific Northwest (PNW) region, with projections to 2009 (APA 2006c).

avoiding the higher cost and relative scarcity of softwood peeler logs required by the plywood industry.

OSB capacity expanded in the United States since its introduction around 1980, with 14.4 billion ft², 3/8-in. basis (billion ft²) of capacity in 2003, but OSB capacity also

expanded in other countries with pulpwood resources suitable for OSB production, primarily Canada (10.8 billion ft²), Europe (3.5 billion ft²), and Latin America (0.5 billion ft²) (APA 2003; RISI 2003; Wood Based Panels International 2005). Although the United States still has the largest share of softwood plywood capacity (16 billion ft², down from a peak of 24 billion ft² around 1990), Latin American softwood plywood capacity doubled since 1990 (to around 4.9 billion ft² in 2003), and Canadian capacity also increased slightly in recent years (to around 2.3 billion ft²).

Softwood plywood was not only displaced from the North American structural wood panel market by OSB, but U.S. softwood plywood also lost its former global leadership position in offshore wood panel markets. As structural wood panel production shifted from softwood plywood to OSB, and both OSB and plywood capacity expanded internationally, U.S. softwood plywood exports dropped precipitously, particularly in the 1990s. With displacement of the formerly dominant position of U.S. softwood plywood in structural panel markets over the course of just two decades since the early 1980s, the United States shifted from being self-sufficient and the leading global exporter of wood panel products to being the world's leading importer. By 2005, it was apparent that the continued downturn entailed the loss of most U.S. export markets for structural wood panels and a structural shift toward increased reliance on imports as depicted in Figures 38 to 40.

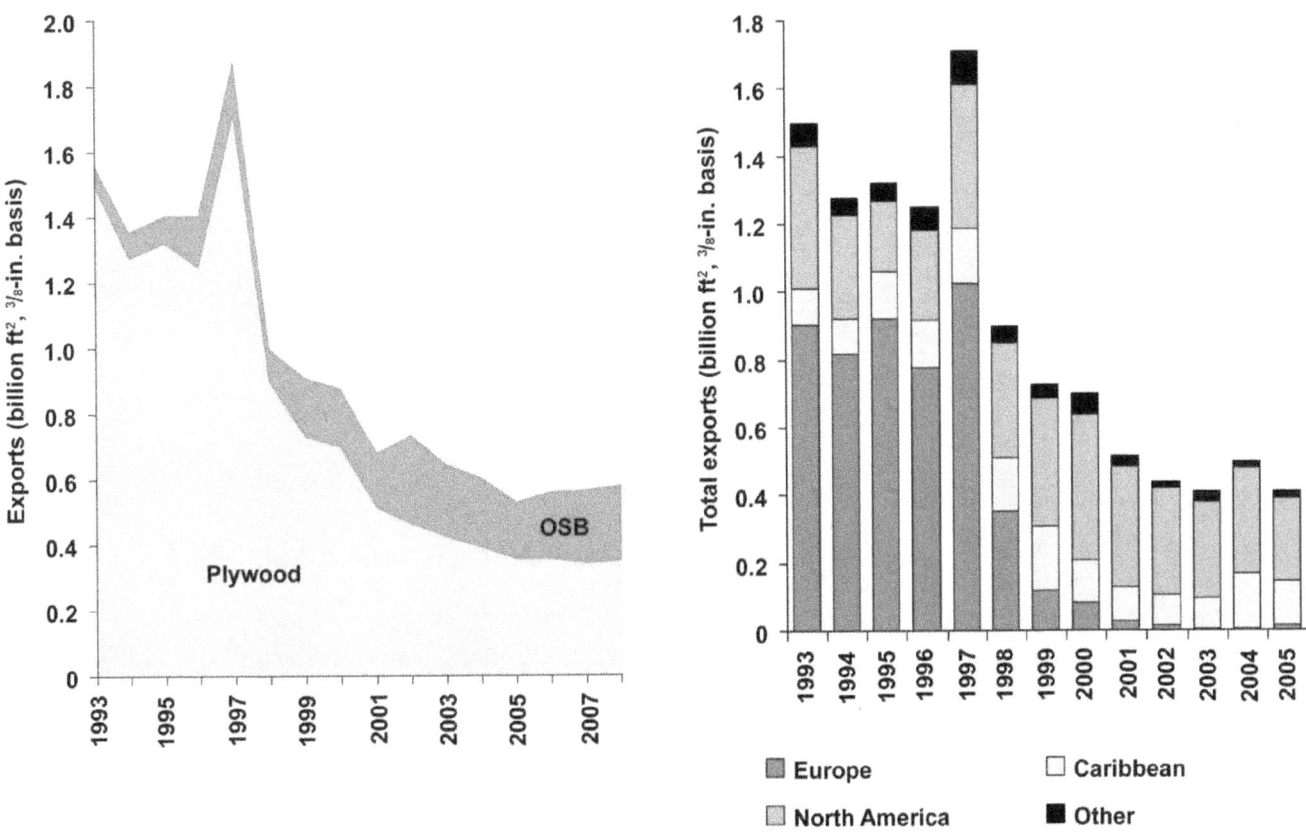

Figure 38—Trends in U.S. structural wood panel exports—oriented strandboard (OSB) and plywood (APA 2006a).

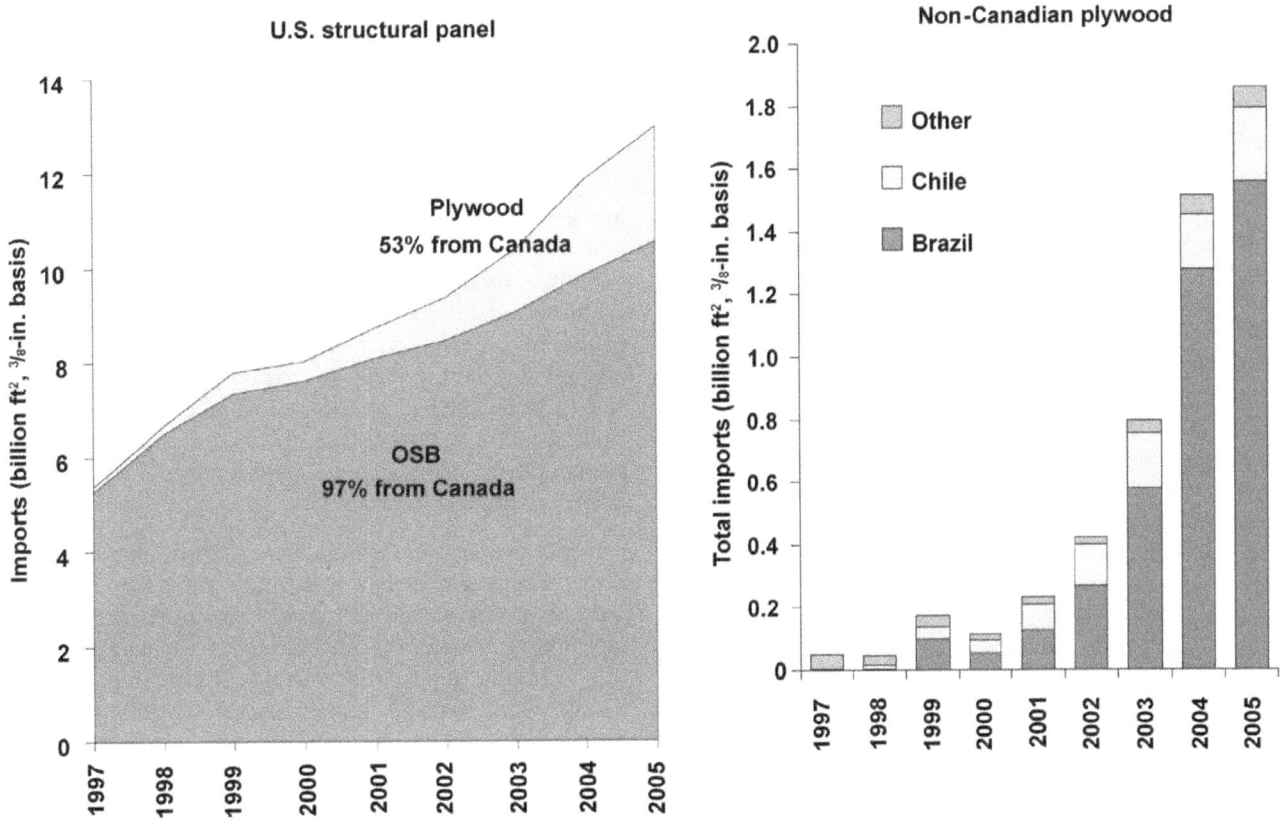

Figure 39—Trends in U.S. structural wood panel imports, climbing to 30% of U.S. structural panel needs—mostly from Canadian oriented strandboard (OSB) but also from elsewhere (plywood) (APA 2006b).

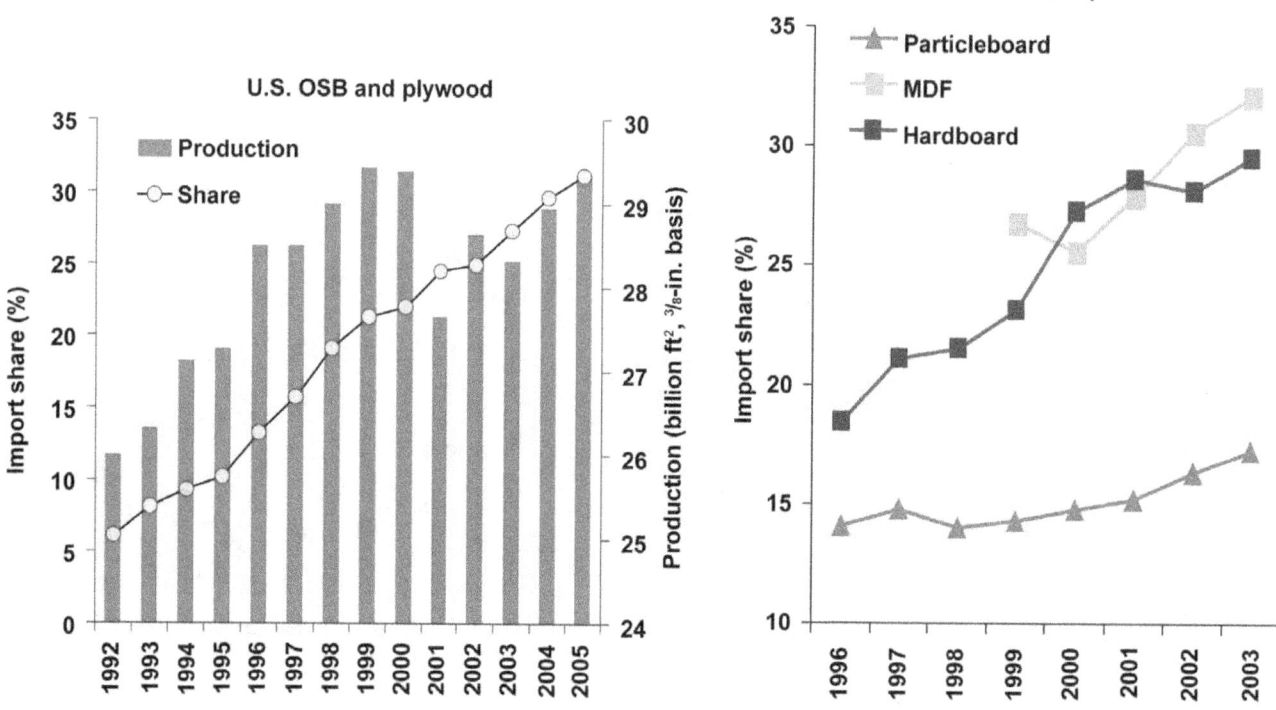

Figure 40—Trends in U.S. import market shares of consumption for wood panels—roughly 25% of the overall wood panel market and growing APA (2006b). Right graph, RISI (2004a).

Competitive Position and Response

The competitive position of structural wood panel producers is determined primarily by wood raw material costs, and secondarily by capital costs, labor costs, and exogenous factors such as currency exchange rates. For U.S. producers of OSB, wood raw material represents around 41% of production costs, and for softwood plywood 50% of production costs (RISI 2003a). That is not as high as for lumber (where wood is estimated to be 66% of production costs), but wood is nevertheless the biggest element of production costs for structural wood panels (OSB and softwood plywood). This means that the competitive position of each producer is heavily influenced by relative cost of wood raw material inputs, and the United States no longer has the clear competitive cost advantage it once had in Douglas-fir plywood production. In 2003, the delivered price of logs suitable for structural softwood plywood was reportedly around 20% lower in New Zealand and Eastern Canada than in the U.S. South or PNW region, and less than half as expensive in Brazil, while the delivered price of pulpwood suitable for OSB was lower in New Zealand, Indonesia, and Brazil than in the United States (WRI 2004).

Nonstructural wood panel products, such as interior-grade particleboard, MDF, and hardboard are made mostly from wood residues (primarily byproducts of sawmills such as wood chips, slabs, sawdust, and other residues). Wood residues tend to be cheaper than roundwood and are relatively abundant in the U.S. forest product sector and also in other leading lumber producing regions of the world. Thus, wood raw material costs are relatively less important in nonstructural wood panel products than labor or capital costs. Note that OSB plants are also generally more capital-intensive and have lower wood raw material costs than plywood mills, but the United States also lacks distinct competitive advantage in labor or capital costs.

Thus, the North American wood panel industry has pursued competitive advantage via twin strategies of mill efficiency improvement and consolidation. Efficiency was pursued primarily via economies of scale and increased capital intensity, with firms operating plants that were ever larger, more automated, and increasingly efficient. Consolidation led to closure of older and less efficient mills. Figure 41 illustrates net results of these strategies in terms of historical increases in average production capacities of wood panel plants in North America, including OSB, MDF, and particleboard plants, with a notable decrease in the number of wood panel mills in operation.

Paradoxical effects of increased scale, capital intensity, and higher productivity include fewer mills, fewer jobs at mills, and a tendency toward lower commodity prices when excess capacity is available, as economies of scale reduce marginal costs of production. Extended periods of low prices and excess capacity typically lead to limited capacity growth and rollbacks in production, which make the market prone to greater price volatility whenever demand shifts upward again. Thus, as shown in Figure 42, the U.S. wood panel composite price exhibited a generally declining tendency through a period of excess capacity from 1999 until early

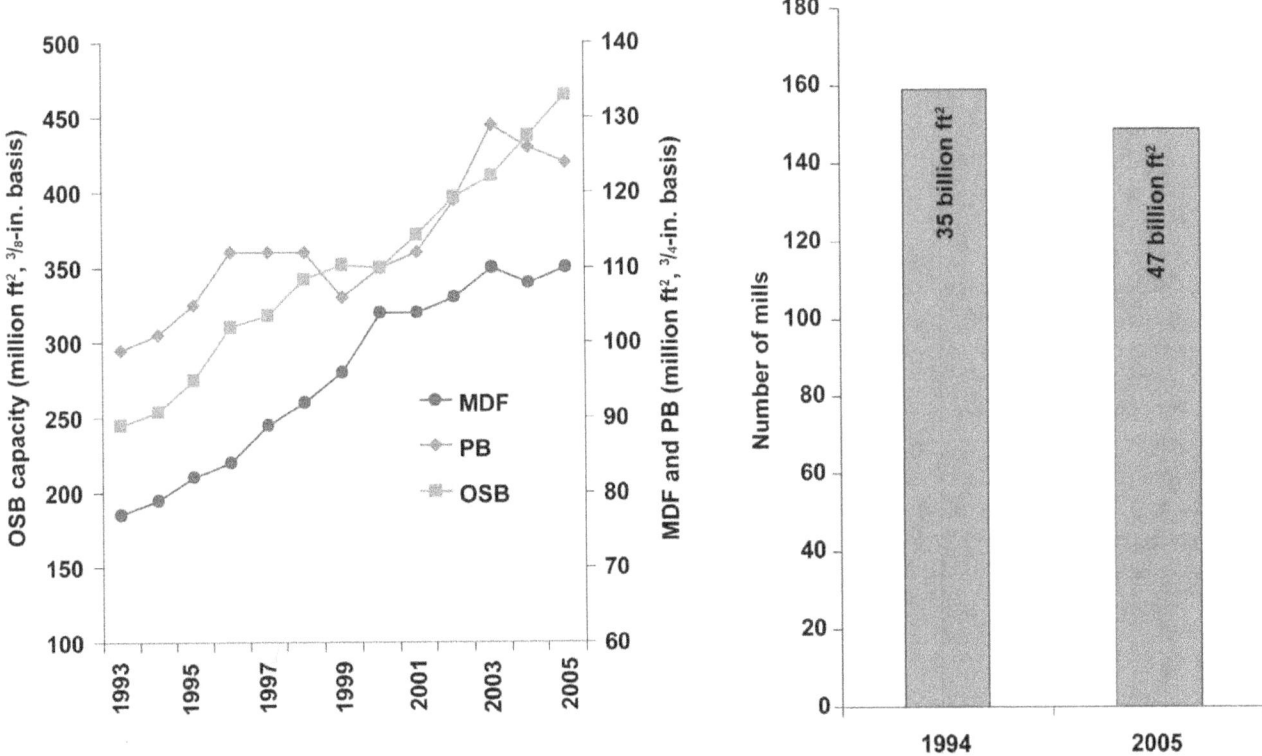

Figure 41—Trend in average plant capacity for oriented strandboard (OSB), medium density fiberboard (MDF), and particleboard mills in North America (U.S. and Canada), and number and capacity of wood structural panel mills (RISI 2004a).

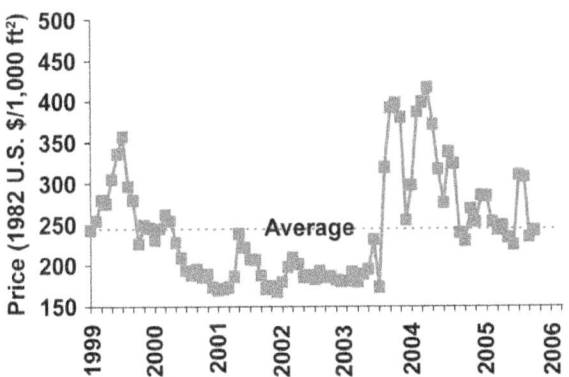

Figure 42—Trend in U.S. wood panel composite price index, 1999–2004 (Random Lengths 2006).

The strategy of efficiency improvement through larger scale and more automated production facilities was pursued not only in the United States but also in other countries such as Canada and more recently in countries such as Brazil. When panel prices spike upward, as they did in 2003, leading producers reap the benefits of larger scale production facilities. However, the market also tends to experience extended periods of excess capacity, with prices lower than average for those periods. Although prices have spiked well above the average on at least two occasions in the past 7 years, the average price is nevertheless much closer to the lower end of the price spectrum (Fig. 42). A drop in housing demand in 2006 has resulted in excess capacity again, with wood panel prices dropping back toward marginal costs of production, as they did following the previous price spike in 1999.

What else can be done? Developing new markets and applications for wood panel products is one strategic adjunct to efficiency improvement and industry consolidation. One view is that new products and new building systems are needed to expand markets for U.S. wood panel producers, but the essential issue will remain whether U.S. producers will be competitive, either in new or existing markets. Globalization, technology change, and consolidation have made wood panel markets more competitive, eroding the once dominant position of U.S. plywood producers in global markets. Export markets were lost for most commodity grades of structural and nonstructural panels. In addition, some key

2003, and then a dramatic price spike occurred as demand surged in the context of limited capacity growth in 2003–2004. The wood panel price spike occurred when surging housing demand and increased government purchases of wood panels (related to construction in the Middle East) met limited capacity growth, which caused a quick evaporation of excess capacity and led to a sellers' market, testing buyers' marginal willingness to pay. Although OSB experienced price volatility and dramatic inflationary tendencies with limited capacity growth since 1999, the real price of pulpwood (the primary raw material for OSB) experienced a general decline along with real prices for paper and paperboard (Fig. 20).

building material markets are now at a "mature stage" of their product life cycle, and thus more susceptible to substitution and loss of markets both domestic and offshore.

In general, wood panels and traditional building materials such as lumber are losing their traditional shares of the housing material market to newer products—engineered wood products and components (such as wood I-joists, laminated veneer lumber, and trusses) and non-wood products. Engineered wood products are made from the same type of material as lumber and wood panels (OSB, lumber, and laminated veneer), but generally the utilization of wood is more efficient per unit of construction (e.g., per 1,000 ft² of housing). Builders are adopting newer technologies to deal with issues such as skilled labor shortages, site waste, and quality of wood building materials. Efficiency improvements in housing construction include expanded use of prefabricated components such as trusses and prefabricated wall panels (Fig. 43). Wood-frame construction technology has also been losing a small but growing share of the U.S. housing construction market to newer concrete- and steel-framing systems.

From a forest resource perspective, expansion of OSB led to increased use of small trees in wood panel mills and a more diverse range of species use in the eastern United States and Canada (regions where most OSB capacity was built), but similar enhancement of resource use did not occur in the U.S. West. In the West, a few small OSB plants were operating in the early 1990s, but those plants (along with many plywood plants) were shut down in the face of competition from larger OSB plants elsewhere. Meanwhile, dense stands of small-diameter timber still crowd public timberlands in the West, creating fire hazards and a need for thinning or removal of small trees. Harvest and transport costs for such trees in the West, however, are higher than roundwood procurement costs in other regions.

With chronic labor shortages in Japan, many builders there have been compelled to shift from traditional post-and-beam construction to use of more efficient engineered wood products. Thus, U.S. log exports to Japan have declined over the past decade while output of wood panels in Japan has increased. However, OSB export from the U.S. West to Japan is nonexistent, and it is uncertain whether large-scale globally competitive OSB plants could ever be located in the U.S. West, given the large capital requirements and need to ensure stable, low-cost wood supply for such large facilities. In general, maintaining healthy well-managed forests depends on having a healthy and diverse forest product industry, but globalization raises challenging issues in regions such as the U.S. West.

Globalization and Forest Enterprise Development

Forest management opportunities are evolving along with forest enterprise development and economic

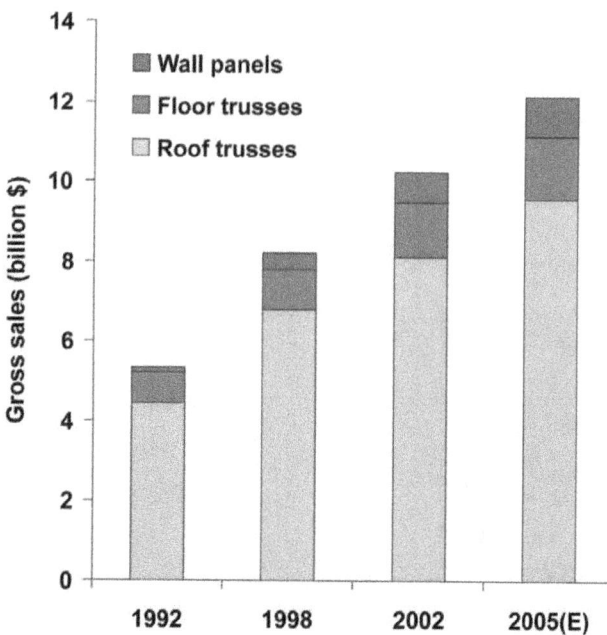

Figure 43—Gross sales of prefabricated wall panels, floor trusses, and roof trusses (WTCA 2002).

globalization, and therefore this section of the report considers how globalization, consolidation, and structural change in the forest sector have broadly shaped forest enterprise development. Previous sections focused on the proposition that economic globalization hastened the process of consolidation and structural change in the overall economy and in forest product markets in particular. Evidence indicated that competitive processes were accelerated by globalization as increased imports of goods stimulated capacity expansion abroad and led to overcapacity, reduced profits, increased cost competition, and consolidation in manufacturing and in forest products. As import competition increased, particularly from low-income countries, observable structural changes included declining U.S. industrial output, shifts in production capacity to low-income countries, cost cutting through outsourcing, and significant reductions in U.S. manufacturing labor input. After increasing for much of the previous century, U.S. output of products such as wood pulp and wood furniture peaked in the mid to late 1990s, and then declined in recent years along with overall U.S. industrial output.

A key hypothesis examined in this section is that economic globalization and import competition also favored survival of U.S. forest product enterprises that are more capital- and skill-intensive, and generally more automated and technologically advanced. This is about survival of the fittest in an era of rising import competition from low-wage countries. The hypothesis is approached first by looking at recent data for leading forest product sectors discussed in previous sections, including pulp and paper, wood panels, softwood lumber, and furniture. These sectors subtend a spectrum of enterprises that range from the more capital-intensive (pulp and paper mills and wood panel mills) to less capital-intensive or more labor-intensive enterprises (sawmills and furniture plants). The hypothesis is tested by examining what happened to the domestically produced market shares of consumption for those products (versus the import market shares) during the recent period of increased import competition, examining whether the more capital-intensive enterprises retained higher market shares.

The hypothesis is suggested by past research into broader effects on U.S. manufacturing of import competition from low-income countries. The past research showed rather clearly that in the period from the early 1970s to late 1990s, imports of goods from low-income countries were the fastest growing component of overall U.S. trade, increasing far more rapidly than total imports, and that this import competition resulted in reallocation of capital among U.S. manufacturing enterprises in general (Bernard and others 2002). The broad reallocation involved shifting toward more capital- and skill-intensive industries in response to low-wage import competition. The research showed that this was accomplished through the processes of plant closure (with more plant closures and less growth among less capital-intensive and less skill-intensive plants), by plant expansion (with higher growth among the more capital-intensive or skill-intensive plants), and by product changes (with plants switching to products or sectors that were more capital-intensive or skill-intensive than industries they left behind).

As explained in preceding sections of this report, the recent period since the early 1990s witnessed profound structural changes in forest product markets under the influence of economic globalization, including an historic downturn in wood pulp production and pulpwood consumption, emergence of a large trade imbalance in the wood panel sector, increased imports of softwood lumber, and significant loss of market share to imports for U.S. household furniture manufacturers. Thus, it is appropriate in this context to consider relative shifts that occurred in the domestically produced shares of consumption for each of those sectors over the period since 1990, as indicators of how well manufacturers in those sectors withstood effects of globalization, consolidation, and structural change. Figure 44 shows data for 1990 and 2002 on domestically produced shares of U.S. consumption for (1) paper and paperboard, (2) OSB and plywood, (3) softwood lumber, and (4) household furniture.

The data (Fig. 44) show that the domestically produced shares of U.S. consumption declined across all four sectors between 1990 and 2002, as import shares of consumption generally increased in all sectors, but the more capital-intensive industries such as pulp and paper and structural wood panels retained generally higher shares of the U.S. market. Meanwhile market shares fell to lower levels for the less capital-intensive or more labor-intensive industries such as sawmills and furniture plants. The OSB and plywood sector experienced a significant shift in market share,

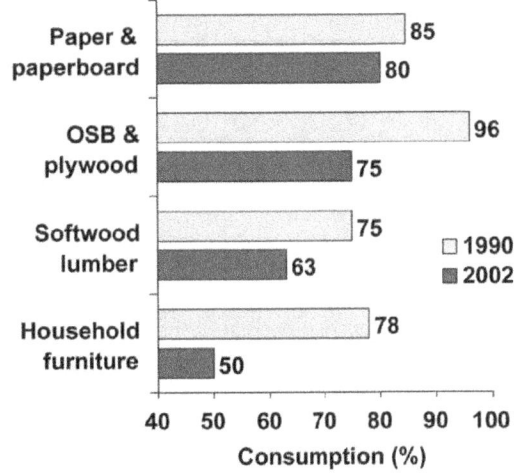

Figure 44—Domestically produced shares of U.S. consumption in four leading forest product sectors, 1990 and 2002.

but that was mainly associated with loss of market share by softwood plywood, which is itself less capital-intensive than OSB.

The trend in enterprise development, favoring survival of more capital-intensive enterprises, reflects also prevailing business strategies. In recent years, U.S. forest product firms pursued strategies of consolidation, automation, and global enterprise development, while seeking also product differentiation, customization, or niche markets as a refuge from volatile global commodity markets. These are parallel strategies, since increased automation and computerization can afford more flexibility and product quality control, which can enable better product differentiation and customer service. Observed differences (Fig. 44) also reflect different levels of success in controlling costs, such as labor costs or wood costs. For example, the U.S. pulp and paper industry faced increased global competition in recent years but was able to control fiber costs partly because of more flexible sourcing of wood fiber (due to increased recycling and greater flexibility in species utilization). Also, labor costs were controlled by process automation and productivity gains. Even within sectors that lost significant market shares to imports, such as wood furniture, surviving plants were generally more automated and less labor intensive.

Figure 45 shows the historical trend in average output capacity of wood pulp mills in the United States back to the early 20th century (Smith and others 2003). The average capacity of U.S. pulp mills has consistently increased, with well-established economies of scale in terms of capital input. Concepts such as the paper "mini mill" and development of niche markets were popularized in recent years; nevertheless, the population of smaller mills has continued to decline, especially in recent years. By 2003, the average capacity of pulp mills in the United States was approaching a thousand tons per day. With lumber and wood panel mill

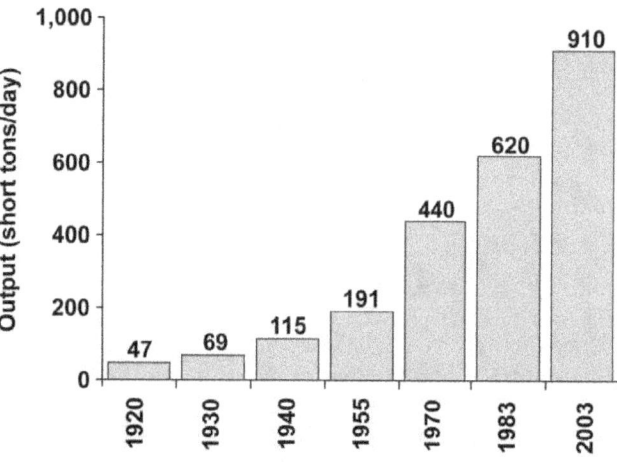

Figure 45—Historical trend in average output capacity of U.S. wood pulp mills.

capacities also increasing (Figs. 32 and 41), the general conclusion is that globalization has favored the continued shift toward larger and more capital-intensive enterprises across the entire forest product sector, generally in the direction of more automated, more efficient, and more globally competitive enterprises. Larger mills can represent investments of hundreds of millions of dollars, which further adds incentive for firms to keep their largest and most efficient mills in operation. The trends are consistent with research observations showing a general shift toward higher capital intensity for overall U.S. manufacturing in the face of import competition (Bernard and others 2002).

Efficiency and product quality gains obtained through more automated or computerized control of manufacturing processes generally favor larger scale or more capital-intensive operations, while also facilitating more flexible systems for design, production, and delivery of goods. Research shows clearly that large- and medium-sized U.S. wood product companies outrun small companies in technology leadership, particularly in process innovation (Wagner and Hanson 2004). This makes it increasingly difficult for small-scale enterprises to compete successfully in most forest product markets, even in the area of customized products or niche markets. Development of customized products and niche markets is a fairly common business strategy even for larger firms. Thus, the numbers of small-scale forest product enterprises have continued to decline in recent years. At present, small-scale enterprises account for only a very small fraction of industrial wood use in the United States. Table 3 provides estimates of U.S. forest product production, roundwood use, and shares of production in small-scale enterprises (including household, farm, ranch, or hobby-scale enterprises and small-scale businesses with less than three employees). As indicated in the table, small-scale enterprises accounted for an estimated 9% of total wood use in 2002, but most of that was fuel wood. Small-scale wood product enterprises accounted for only about 1% of industrial wood use.

In hardwood lumber production, for example, small-scale enterprises once accounted for a fairly significant share of production (perhaps as much as 15% of production as recently as 1970), but U.S. hardwood sawmills have drifted over time toward larger scale and more capital-intensive enterprises. Market demand for better quality hardwood lumber favors improved quality control and investment in advanced computer-controlled equipment. The more automated equipment yields greater product value, but it is more expensive, pushing hardwood sawmills in the direction of more capital-intensive and larger scale enterprises. Other factors pushing the trend toward larger scale hardwood sawmills in recent decades included more robust transportation systems with larger capacity log trucks, and also more abundant volumes of hardwood timber in U.S. forests.

Over the past decade, wood furniture suppliers in the United States found it economical to outsource to low-wage countries the production of more labor-intensive wood furniture components, such as carved wooden components. More recently, it became common to outsource the entire furniture production and assembly process, as production plants were built in low-wage countries. Increased imports of wood furniture provide evidence that innovations in communication, computing, and product distribution facilitate efficient design, production, and delivery of goods from foreign producers. In that context, global electronic communication networks, computerized design, and modern distribution systems have accelerated design, production, and delivery of goods, such that foreign firms or subsidiaries in other countries often have the means to produce custom-ordered products or to exploit niche markets just as quickly or efficiently as local producers. Local small-scale enterprise development in the forest sector is confined primarily to fuel wood production, which has relatively low market value, and to some niche opportunities in small-scale sawmills or post and pole manufacturing. For the most part, it appears that larger scale global markets and global enterprise development will increasingly influence U.S timber markets, rather than smaller scale local or regional market developments.

Trends suggest that future enterprise development in the U.S. forest sector will continue in the direction of larger or global enterprise development, with increased efficiency and automation, generally favoring globally robust and capital-intensive enterprises. At the same time, consolidation in recent years resulted also in a general abatement of growth in timber demand across the entire U.S. forest product sector. The ongoing shift toward global enterprise development along with abatement of growth in U.S. timber demand, even if transitory, has implications for forest stewardship and forest management in the United States.

The abatement of growth in U.S. timber demand and shift toward global enterprise development contributed to an excess of timber growth over removals, at present and in the foreseeable future, with projected expansion of U.S. timber

Table 3—United States forest product production, corresponding roundwood use, and estimated shares of production in small-scale enterprises, including household, farm, ranch, hobby-scale, or small-scale businesses with less than three employees[a]

Forest product category	Total U.S. production, 2002 (million short tons, air dry)	Roundwood use in production (million ft^3)	Production shares (%)
Lumber industry			
Softwood lumber	35.6	5,246	~2
Hardwood lumber[b]	21.6	2,056	~3
Wood panel and veneer industry			
Plywood and LVL	10.7	1,067	0
OSB	8.4	560	0
Particleboard, MDF	8.5	290	0
Insulating board and hardboard	1.8		
Pulp, paper, and paperboard industry[c]	95.9	4,849[d]	0
Other wood product industries[e]	5.2	317	~10
Fuel wood	26.6	1,520	>80
Raw wood exports			
Logs	6.0	388	0
Wood chips	3.5	189	0
Totals:	223.8	16,483	~9 (~1% of industrial wood)

[a]LVL, laminated veneer lumber, MDF, medium density fiberboard; OSB, Oriented strandboard. Production and roundwood use data from Howard 2003b. Small enterprise shares of production are best-guess estimates.
[b]Hardwood lumber includes lumber made from roundwood at pallet mills.
[c]Pulp, paper, and paperboard includes total U.S. production of paper and paperboard, plus U.S. market pulp production for export.
[d]In addition, 34.6 million tons of recovered (recycled) paper and 1,887 million ft^3 of wood residues were consumed in pulp, paper, and board.
[e]Other industrial wood products include poles, posts, shingle bolts, cooperage, round timbers, chemical wood, and miscellaneous products.

growing stock inventories for decades to come (according to the 2001 RPA timber assessment (RPA 2001), Fig. 19). The excess of U.S. timber growth over timber harvest adds to a broader phenomenon across the entire northern hemisphere, since timber growth exceeds harvest volume by even wider margins in Europe and in Russia. In Russia, timber growth exceeds harvest by a factor of about 5 to 1 (FAO 2001). This suggests, if anything, that timber supplies will be adequate to meet projected demands for decades to come, particularly given the trend toward global enterprise development.

These observations are not intended to downplay the importance of carefully considering forest stewardship and forest management priorities in securing well-managed forests for future generations, but rather to suggest that economic globalization and market development are factors that must be considered in developing support for local forest management activities and in some cases may necessitate re-evaluation of local forest management priorities. The challenge of limited support for forestry activities implies also a need to more carefully allocate limited forest management resources.

Even though survival of more capital-intensive and globally robust enterprises was favored in recent years, the past decade or so was also a period when many large U.S. forest product firms divested millions of acres of timberland as profitability of firms and the rate of appreciation in timberland values subsided (NCREIF 2006). Concurrently, the numbers of U.S. forestry students enrolled at leading universities and membership in professional forestry associations peaked in the 1990s and then declined, coinciding with nationwide declines in timber output such as declining pulpwood receipts at wood pulp mills since the mid-1990s (Fig. 17). Along with notable declines in forest industry employment and gross economic output of forestry in the United States (Fig. 21), these trends suggest that forestry employment and sustainable forest management are suffering from some degree of subordination in the broader context of economic globalization. Priorities of sustainable forest management may be only partially complementary to the drivers of global enterprise development, such as higher profitability, cost competitiveness, market development, or economic efficiency. If so, the challenge of promoting relevance of forestry will increase, and it will become all the more important to study and understand evolving resource opportunities in order to more efficiently match limited development support in forestry to actual economic and social needs.

Opportunities Evolving with Global Supply, Demand, and Trade

Forest resource management and sustainable development opportunities are evolving along with globalization of forest resource supply, forest product demand, and trade. This section discusses examples of how global trends influence broad opportunities in forest management and forest sector development, including the opportunity to restore native or natural forests through development of wood fiber plantations, the opportunity to expand export of wood chips, the opportunity to expand recovery of paper for recycling, and the opportunity for continued development of the U.S. pulp and paper sector.

One evolving opportunity is to continue shifting future expansion of timber harvest from vast areas of native or natural forests to more highly concentrated and productive timber plantations that occupy smaller land areas. According to the recent United Nations FAO Forest Resource Assessment (FAO 2001), the world's total area of land with forest or tree cover is 3.9 billion hectares, or 30% of the world's land surface area, somewhat less than one hectare of land (~2 acres) with tree cover per capita worldwide (FRA 2003). According to FRA 2003, by far the vast majority of that area is native forest of natural origin, but a small fraction of land area with tree cover consists of tree plantations, where native or exotic trees have been planted on forestland or on previously non-forested areas.

According to FRA 2003, plantations accounted for 5% of global land area with tree cover, but only a fraction of tree plantations are industrial wood plantations (most tree plantations serve other purposes such as soil conservation, or cultivation of crops such as fruits, nuts, or extractives, such as rubber tree plantations). According to more recent estimates based partly on FRA 2003, fast-growing industrial wood plantations occupy just 2% of forested land area worldwide, yet they supply one quarter of all industrial roundwood (Siry and others 2003). Furthermore, plantations are projected to supply half of global wood resource needs within two decades (Poyry 1999). In addition, the 2001 RPA timber assessment projected that softwood timber supply from managed plantations in the United States (primarily Southern Pine plantations) will climb to more than half of total softwood timber supply; yet managed plantations were projected to increase from only 6% of U.S. timberland area to about 9% by the year 2050 (Haynes 2003). Most of the projected increase in U.S. timber supply is accounted for by plantations, and not by natural forests.

Environmentalists have criticized industrial wood plantations, which they view as monocultures that lack species diversity. Also, plantations may occupy sites formerly occupied by more biologically diverse native forest cover (Mattoon 1998). However, in many forested areas, such as in the U.S. South for example, plantations of varying age are interspersed with native forest stands, resulting in a mosaic of varied forest cover types and somewhat diverse habitat for wildlife species. Also, pine plantations were historically established on marginal agricultural land. In any case, industrial plantations occupy only a small fraction of forested land area nationwide (6%) or worldwide (2%).

Although industrial wood plantations tend not to be favored by environmentalists, some advocates of industrial ecology have noted that wood output from highly productive plantations may reduce or offset timber harvest on the broader expanses of native or natural forest areas. The term "Great Restoration" has been applied to the general idea that relatively small areas of managed plantations coupled with other conservation measures permit continued restoration of native forests over large areas (Victor and Ausubel 2000; Victor 2003). Restoration of forests has been ongoing in the United States for decades, as evidenced by expansion of timber growing stock inventory (Fig. 19)—benefiting from previously established plantations, more efficient wood use, recycling, and increased wood product imports. Furthermore, pressures of increased timber harvest on U.S. timberlands have leveled off in recent years mainly because of globalization, consolidation, and abatement of growth in various U.S. forest product sectors (discussed earlier).

Whereas harvest on timber plantations may offset timber harvest on other forest lands, economic globalization also affects incentives for development of plantations. Timber demand is a primary incentive for technological development in forestry, such as tree cultivation and genetic selection, and for investment in commercial tree plantations. As noted earlier, economic globalization contributed to declining U.S. pulpwood demand and pulpwood prices (Figs. 17 and 20), with declining profitability in the U.S. pulp and paper sector (Fig. 13) and significant divestitures of timberland holdings by many forest product firms in recent years. Given those trends, it becomes questionable whether financial support for technological development and investment in wood fiber plantations will continue to be available in the future. In recent years there is evidence of reductions in the rate of pine plantation establishment in the U.S. South, with reduced orders for pine seedlings at tree nurseries. In the long run, productivity gains of timber plantations may be hampered by declines in tree planting or plantation management, particularly in the U.S. South. However, because growth in U.S. timber harvest in recent years has significantly moderated (Fig. 18), timber harvest in U.S. native or natural forests has declined. This decline has been partly a result of increased harvest on established plantations as well as economic globalization.

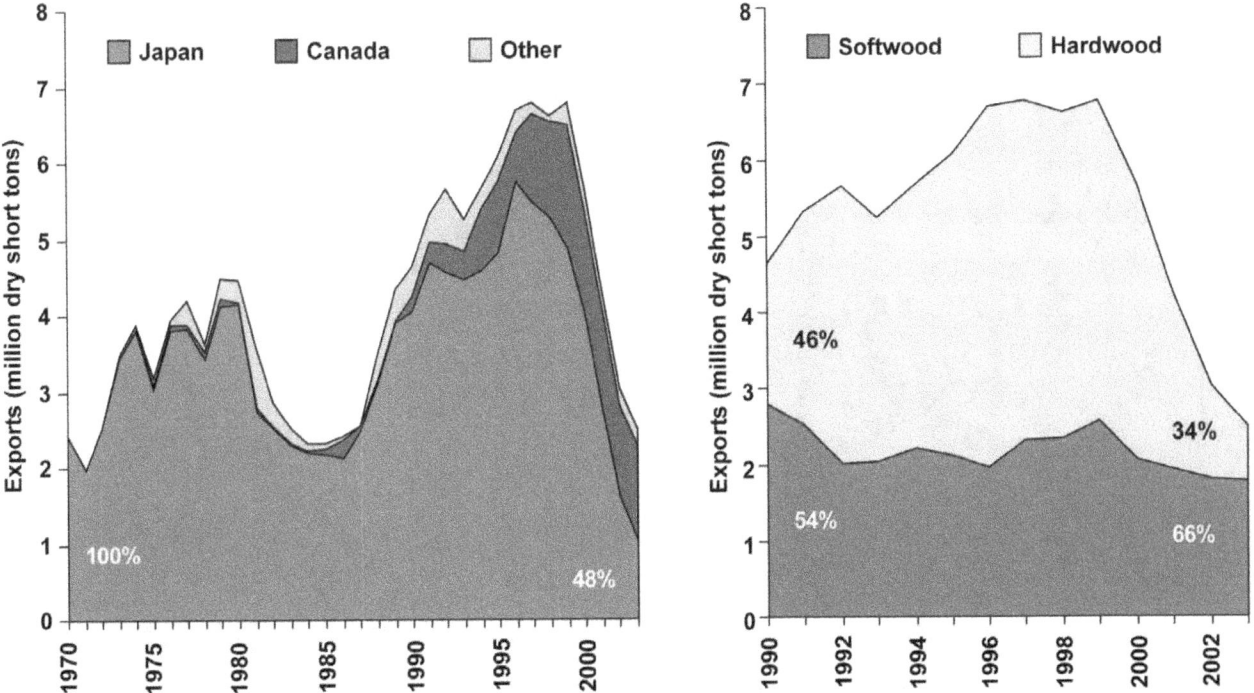

Figure 46—Historical trends in U.S. exports of wood chips by export destination, 1970–2003, and by species group, 1990–2003. Left and right graph, U.S. Department of Commerce data in U.S. International Trade Commission database (2004).

Meanwhile, regions of Asia and Latin America continue to experience expansion in wood fiber plantations (particularly hardwoods such as eucalyptus and acacia). Overseas expansion of plantations has displaced U.S. exports of wood chips, particularly exports of hardwood chips from the U.S. South. Some buyers of pulp and paper products have also begun to demand products that do not use wood chips from "old growth" forests, or to demand environmentally certified forest products, trends that favor sourcing of wood chips from fiber plantations.

Figure 46 shows historical trends in U.S. exports of wood chips. Japan was historically the leading export destination for U.S. wood chips, but exports to Japan fell dramatically since the mid-1990s, as Japan increased imports of wood chips from other countries and the exchange value of the dollar increased from 1996 to 2002. United States wood chip exports also dropped in the mid-1980s as the exchange value of the dollar peaked previously during that decade. Although the dollar weakened in 2003, U.S. wood chip exports did not increase. Opportunities to export chips were offset in recent years by increasingly abundant supplies of low-cost fiber from fast-growing eucalyptus plantations in Latin America and Asia, and by expansion in global output of hardwood market pulp (increasingly based on fiber plantations). A further decline in the exchange value of the dollar may restore some opportunity for increased U.S. wood chip export, but ongoing expansions of global wood fiber plantations tend to diminish that opportunity.

Expansion of paper and paperboard production capacity in China has increased Chinese demand for low cost fiber raw material, and many new mills in China have been designed to use recycled fiber. Thus, the opportunity has expanded for the United States to export recovered paper for recycling to China, and in recent years China became the leading destination for U.S. exports of recovered paper. China also has become also the leading global importer of recovered paper for recycling, although in 2004 the cost of transoceanic shipments of all bulk commodities such as recovered paper were affected by a dramatic increase in ocean freight shipping rates. Figure 47 shows the historical trend in disposition of paper recovered for recycling in the United States (domestic use and export) and the trends in U.S. exports of recovered paper by export destination.

Although domestic use of recovered paper for recycling peaked in 1999 along with U.S. paper and paperboard production, U.S. recovery of paper for recycling and exports of recovered paper continued to expand, particularly exports to China. Whereas recycling at domestic paper and paperboard mills once in 1970 accounted for 97% of paper recovered for recycling, nearly one-quarter of all paper recovered for recycling was exported in 2002. China alone accounted for 43% of U.S. recovered paper exports by 2003.

Expansion of the capital intensity and scale of production at forest product facilities in countries like China is another aspect of rapid structural change facilitated by economic globalization. Prior to the 1990s, the vast majority of paper

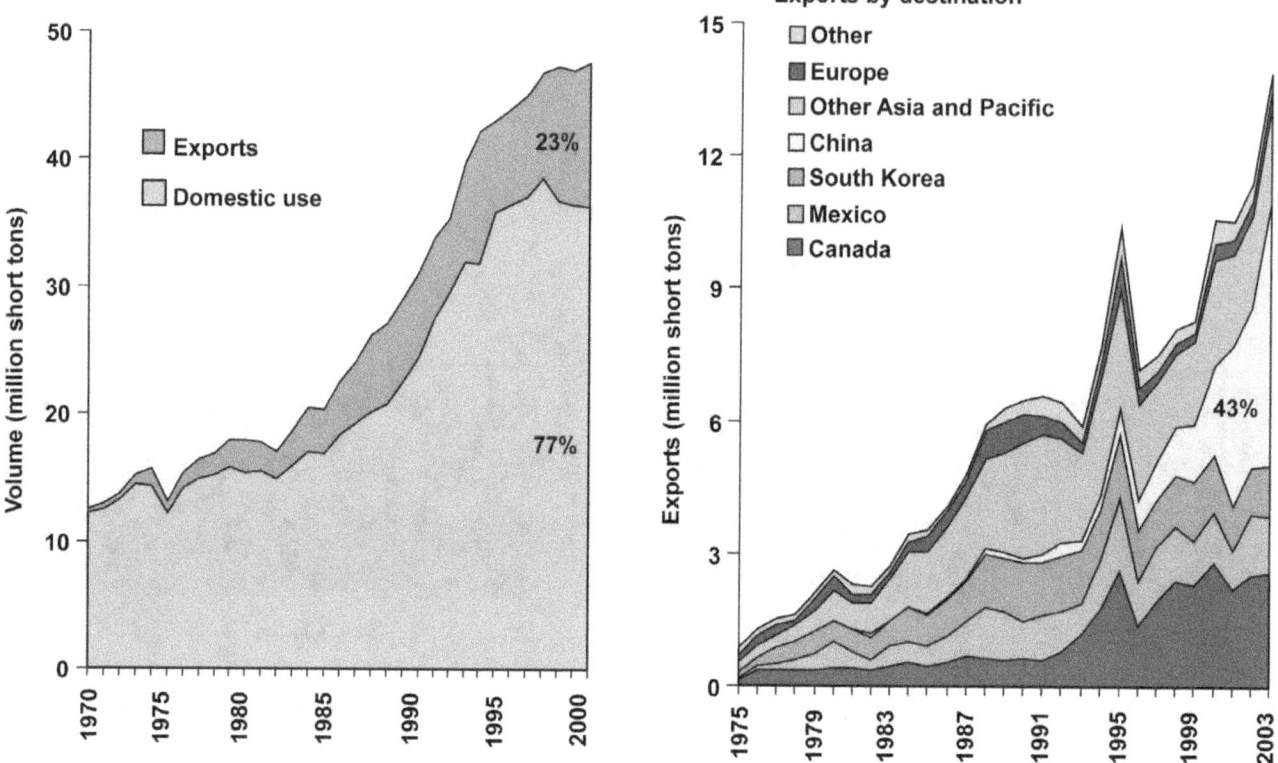

Figure 47—Historical trends in disposition of paper recovered for recycling in the United States and exports of recovered paper by destination (AF&PA 2006).

and paperboard mills in China were very small facilities (by Western standards). RISI (2004b) estimated that as recently as 1995 only about one-third of the newsprint, printing and writing paper, containerboard, and boxboard capacity in China was in mills with capacity greater than 50,000 metric tons per year, but by 2003 nearly 60% of the capacity was in such mills. Large mill projects in China are facilitated by largely unimpeded flows of capital and engineering expertise into China. Pulp and paper engineering and construction firms are global enterprises, and many large mills in China and elsewhere in Asia and Latin America were built in recent years with participation of international firms, mainly from Europe, who introduced the latest expertise, automation, and equipment. Large-scale mills now account for the bulk of Chinese production capacity in paper and paperboard, and some of the largest mills in the world have been built in China in recent years.

In the context of economic globalization and global expansion of pulp, paper, and paperboard capacity as well as wood fiber plantations, U.S. exports of paper and paperboard leveled out and declined over the past decade, as did U.S. exports of wood pulp, as shown in Figure 48. As noted previously, the U.S. trade deficit in pulp, paper, and paperboard products went from less than 1 million tons in 1996 to around 9 million tons in 2003, with trade influenced by the strong U.S. dollar (Fig. 10).

Nevertheless, the United States remains by far the world's leading producer of pulp, paper, and paperboard products (followed by China) and also remains one of the world's leading exporters of those products. Furthermore, although U.S. exports have dropped over the past decade, they have not entirely collapsed (Fig. 48).

The dominant global position of the United States in pulp, paper, and paperboard production coupled with continued significant participation in global markets suggest that there may yet be future opportunities for expansion and growth in the U.S. pulp and paper sector, particularly if the exchange value of the U.S. dollar were to decline further or growth in U.S. industrial output were to recover. The 2001 RPA timber assessment projected a gradual recovery for U.S. pulp and paper output in the years ahead (Figs. 12 and 17). In addition, opportunities for future growth in pulp and paper (as well as other wood product sectors) will likely be affected by lingering effects of globalization and consolidation and by continued expansion of foreign production capacity. Limited U.S. capacity growth of recent years might, for example, amplify inflationary price effects of an upturn in pulp and paper demand in the short run, but capacity growth in low-cost regions abroad might dampen inflationary trends.

Globalization and Sustainable Forest Management

The last hypothesis examined in this report is that globalization and related structural changes altered economic opportunities and pathways for sustainable forest management in the United States. As discussed previously, economic globalization contributed to accelerated structural changes within the forest sector of the United States since the early 1990s, as reflected by downturns over the past decade in the economic value of forestry outputs, forest sector employment, and the contribution of forestry to GDP. Changes were sufficient to alter basic economic, social, and environmental dimensions of forest management, influencing economic feasibility of forest management in the United States. The following sections discuss effects of economic globalization on sustainable forest management from a broad philosophical perspective and also discuss various strategic remedies, which in many cases would extend well beyond the forest sector itself.

The information presented in preceding sections indicated also an evolving relation between economic globalization and the ability to maintain or enhance socioeconomic benefits of sustainable forest management in the United States. Some view economic globalization and sustainable development as competing paradigms, while still others would view them as complementary. Forest policies will be better guided in any case by understanding how economic globalization and sustainable forest management are related, both positively and negatively. This can be facilitated by understanding how economic globalization contributes to structural change in the forest sector, and in turn how structural change in the forest sector affects opportunities for sustainable forest management. In expanding that understanding,

it helps to begin with a simple recognition that economic globalization and sustainable development are generally viewed as separate and distinct philosophical concepts.

Whether or not one accepts or rejects the idea that economic globalization and sustainable development are competing paradigms, the two concepts should at least be viewed as distinct, each having a unique focus and specific context. The focus of economic globalization is commerce, within the context of international rules of commerce (such as free trade policy), global markets, and capitalism. Economic globalization is driven primarily by a universal profit motive, with very limited focus on rules of governance pertaining to the broader dimensions of society or the environment. On the other hand, sustainable development is focused more directly on issues of intergenerational equity and governance, mostly pertaining to social values and the environment, influenced by commerce but with little if any focus on rules of commerce. Popularization of the sustainable development concept is widely attributed to the World Commission on Environment and Development, which offered in 1987 a definition of sustainable development as that which "meets the needs of the present without compromising the ability of future generations to meet their own needs" (World Commission 1987). The idea of sustainable development arose in the context of concerns for the environment and social welfare, motivated by an understanding that the environment and society are affected by commercial economic development and profit-making activities. Figure 49 illustrates the core focus and separate contexts for both of these distinct concepts.

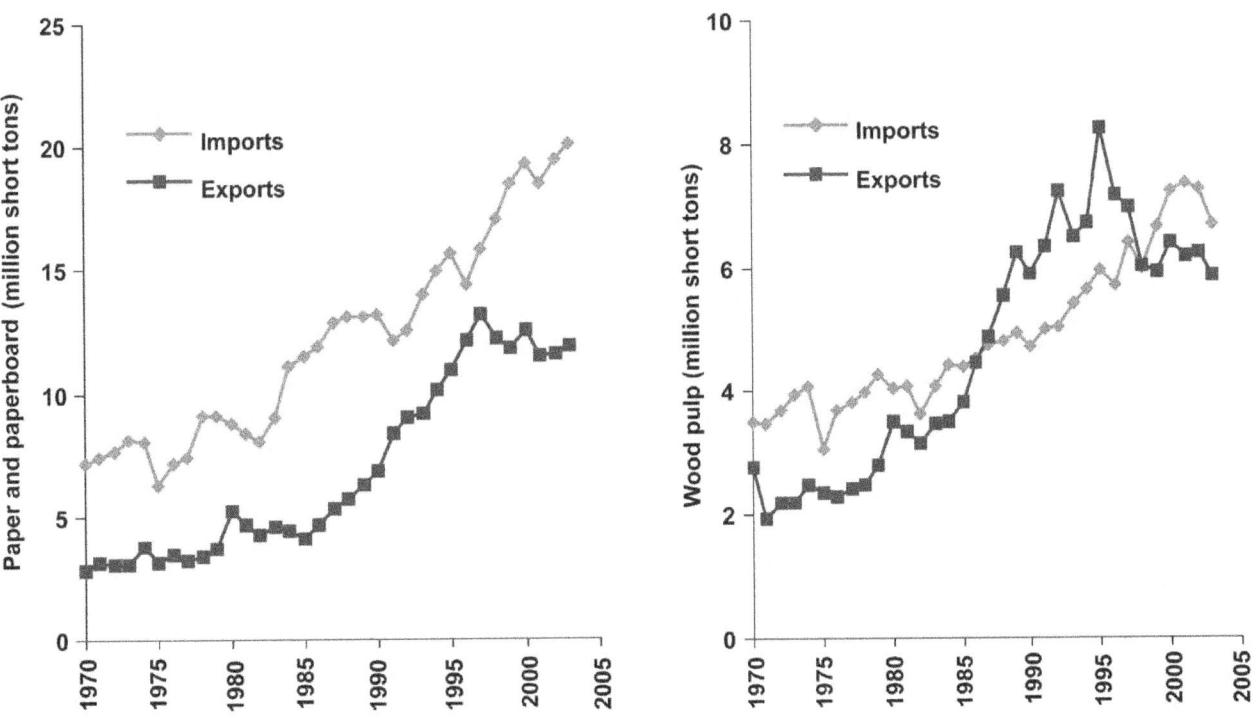

Figure 48—Historical trends in U.S. exports and imports of paper and paperboard (left) and wood pulp (right), 1970–2003 (AF&PA 2006). Paper and board include converted products.

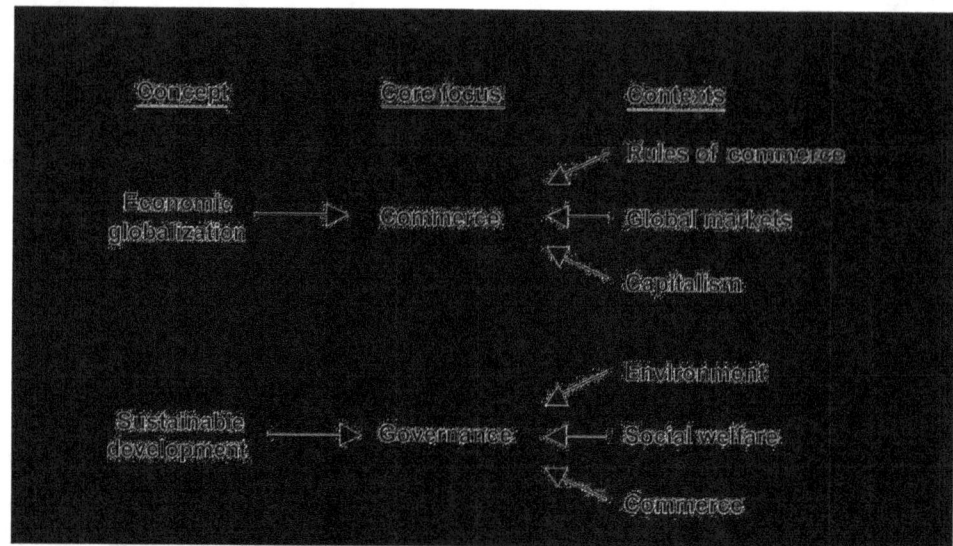

Figure 49—Focus and context of globalization and sustainable development concepts.

One view of economic globalization (and universal push toward greater efficiency via consolidation and structural change) is that important but seemingly less productive objectives of sustainable development (such as environmental or social objectives) may be subordinated by economic globalization, simply because those objectives may not be complementary to profitability, market development, cost competitiveness, or efficiency. For example, rules of commerce and trends in international commerce and trade have reportedly subordinated the environmental objective of maintaining large populations of forest-dependent species such as wild salmon in the Pacific Northwest, simply because the overarching global drive for economic efficiency has marginalized expensive restoration of wild salmon populations (Lackey 2003). In general, objectives such as conservation of biological diversity by preserving wildlife habitat or the promotion of social welfare by providing steady local employment opportunity may become subordinated by the drivers of economic globalization. Subordination of environmental objectives by the forces of economic globalization (e.g,. the drive for economic efficiency and cost reduction) is a subtle variation on a much more general theme—that growth in population, affluence, and technology are driving forces for environmental degradation. The latter paradigm is known as the IPAT model (Impact on environment = Population × Affluence × Technology) attributed to Erlich and Holdren (1972). Affluence and technology can alternatively be viewed as a means of avoiding environmental degradation (by affording to obtain more efficient use of resources).

Indeed, there is also a view that economic efficiency and other structural changes will compensate in the long run for the marginalizing influence of economic globalization. In particular, there is the economic hypothesis that free trade and economic efficiency will provide enormous overall economic benefits to society in the long run, creating wealth and prosperity, such that society will eventually afford to spend more on those activities that are viewed as environmentally or socially important, such as wildlife conservation and community development. Some limited empirical evidence for the "environmental Kuznets curve" discussed previously supports this view.

Therein is the crux of the debate about economic globalization and sustainable development. Will the drivers of globalization and consolidation (profits, market development, cost competitiveness, and economic efficiency) subordinate less productive or less efficient objectives of sustainable development? Or will those drivers contribute in the long run toward greater overall wealth and prosperity such that society will better afford to appreciate and pay the expense of achieving the full set of sustainable development objectives? In the case of the U.S. forest sector at least, it would appear that economic globalization and consolidation of the forest product industry in recent years resulted in structural changes, including reduced employment and reduced timber harvest levels, reduced domestic demands for forest resources, and therefore reduced economic returns associated with sustainable management of forest resources.

International criteria and indicators of sustainable forest management help to facilitate more detailed discussion of sustainable development in the forest sector, exemplified by criteria and indicators developed in the Montréal Process stemming from the 1992 Earth Summit. Some of the criteria and indicators of sustainable forest management are indeed noneconomic or largely unrelated to market development or economic efficiency, and thus one might suspect logically that management objectives related to those indicators might become subordinated by the drivers of globalization and consolidation. However, as explained below, many of the criteria and indicators can be viewed as at least indirectly linked to the ongoing process of economic globalization.

The 1992 Earth Summit in Brazil, or United Nations Conference on Environment and Development (UNCED), called upon all nations to ensure sustainable development, including sustainable development in the management of all types of forests. The summit produced a Statement of Forest Principles; conventions on biodiversity, climate change, and desertification; and a plan of action for the 21st century called Agenda 21, all of which had implications for forest management (Earth Summit 1992).

Following UNCED, Canada convened the International Seminar of Experts on Sustainable Development of Boreal and Temperate Forests. This seminar, which was held in Montréal in 1993 and sponsored by the Conference on Security and Cooperation in Europe, focused specifically on a broad set of criteria and indicators and how they can help define and measure progress towards sustainable development of forests at a national level. The Montréal Process Working Group agreed on a framework of criteria and indicators that provided member countries with a common definition of what characterizes sustainable management of temperate and boreal forests (Montréal Process 1998–2005). The framework identified seven leading criteria that are further defined by 67 associated indicators, which are aspects of the criteria that can be identified or described. Table 4 gives a summary of the Montréal Process Criteria. Furthermore, these efforts gave rise to a generalized concept of sustainable forest management, which generally extends ideals of sustainable development to forest management, although technically sustainable forest management encompasses many issues and lacks a universally accepted definition (Wang 2004).

It becomes readily apparent that the implicit objectives of some of the criteria of sustainable forest management (such as 1, 3, and 5) are only remotely connected to core drivers of economic globalization. Activities related to criteria such as conservation of biological diversity, maintenance of ecosystem health, or maintenance of forest contribution to global carbon cycling, could therefore become subordinated by business decisions and broader government policies focused on the core drivers of globalization and consolidation, such as profits, market development, cost competitiveness, and economic efficiency. Some of the other criteria

(such as 2 and 4) may be positively but indirectly linked to drivers of globalization and consolidation, inasmuch as regional productive capacity of forests or the condition of soil and water resources may influence trends in global economic development, and vice-versa. The remaining criteria (6 and 7) are more or less directly connected to economic globalization and are likely to evolve in direct response to the consequences or priorities of globalization and business consolidation. Nevertheless, effects of globalization and consolidation cut across all Montréal Process Criteria because of their influence on timber harvest.

Crosscutting implications of globalization and consolidation for sustainable forest management will be discussed further, but some additional observations need to be made first about a philosophical dichotomy between economic globalization and the concept of sustainable development. Some scholars have expressed a view that sustainability is simply not an appropriate topic to be discussed by economists, although two entire issues of the journal *Forest Policy and Economics* were devoted recently to "economics of sustainable forest management" (Kant 2004). Issues 3 and 4 of Volume 6 contain 16 papers on the topic. One key observation is that not only the focus and context of both concepts differ (Fig. 49), but also the concept of sustainable development seems to influence how behavioral reality is interpreted among those who subscribe to the concept. For example, Kates wrote in 2003 that the "genius" of the sustainable development concept lies in its essential ambiguity, the oxymoronic juxtaposition of the concepts of sustainability and economic development, which "seeks to finesse the real conflicts between economy and the environment, and between the present and the future." Furthermore, Speth (2003) also wrote that "most analysts now agree that from an environmental perspective, sustainable development requires living off nature's income rather than consuming natural capital."

The two preceding interpretations of sustainable development are superficially different, but they both reflect a much bigger difference in how people may view the reality of human economic behavior. In the first interpretation, all economic development is viewed as incompatible with

Table 4—Montréal Process criteria

Montréal Process criteria	Number of indicators
1. Conservation of biological diversity	9
2. Maintenance of productive capacity of forest ecosystems	5
3. Maintenance of forest ecosystem health	3
4. Conservation and maintenance of soil and water resources	8
5. Maintenance of forest contribution to global carbon cycles	3
6. Maintenance and enhancement of long-term multiple socioeconomic benefits to meet the needs of society	19
7. Legal, institutional and economic framework for forest conservation and sustainable management	20

environmental and social sustainability, at best a mix of oxymoronic concepts, ultimately and mutually exclusive. In the second interpretation, sustainable development is connected philosophically to an economic concept easily recognized by those with a business or fiduciary background, namely the concept of preservation of capital. However, Speth (2003) goes on to say that "In the terminology of the economists, it implies non-declining natural assets at a minimum."

Thus, both preceding interpretations of sustainable development can be contrasted sharply with conventional economic interpretations of human behavior—specifically that economic optimization is the paradigm of modern business behavior (including economic globalization and business consolidation in the forest sector). For example, even if preservation of natural capital was assumed as a primary objective (by imposing the constraint of "living off nature's income" only) there would still be economic options in management of natural capital; thus, economic behavior implies somewhat more than just "non-declining natural assets." In the short run, economic behavior will imply maximization of return on assets, and in the long run it may also imply expansion of investment in profitable assets, not just preservation but also expansion of capital. Furthermore, optimization admits the possibility that there are many options in the course of economic development, some more economical than others. Thus, even if economic behavior and sustainability are viewed as mutually exclusive, the reality of human economic behavior is that it tends to seek the most economical option, which may or may not be more socially or environmentally sustainable than other options.

For example, in forestry it has been understood for a long time that there can be many fully sustainable forest management or silvicultural regimes, but some are more economical than others. This was recognized, for example, in 1849 by the famous German forester, Martin Faustmann, who outlined in that year the modern concept of forest capital valuation, which led also to economic optimization through choice of forest management regime. In his case study, Faustmann assumed that there were many alternative forest management regimes (with varying rotation periods) that could be sustained in perpetuity. In all cases it was assumed that the form of natural capital could be preserved for future generations (through infinite rotations), yet even under such idealized assumptions Faustmann showed how to find which management regime was economically optimal. Even when a forest is managed in an idealized sustainable manner for perpetuity, some management regimes are simply more economical than others, in terms of economic or social benefits and costs.

Faustmann's concept of economic optimization is still relevant in modern forestry (Chang 1998), although some would prefer to focus on preservation of natural capital in its native form, rather than focus on how to manage those assets most economically. On the other hand, business behavior and economic globalization are all about how to manage assets in order to maximize profit. Whether or not the original form of the capital is preserved, enhanced, or liquidated may be a subordinate concern. Thus, interpretations of the concept of sustainable development can influence views of behavioral imperatives. Foresters such as Faustmann may have assumed that forests would be managed in perpetuity with infinite rotations (preserving forever the form and productivity of natural forest capital), but global economic behavior and global businesses tend to focus more on managing capital to maximize profits, income, and wealth.

The philosophical divergence in viewpoints about objectives of managing natural capital (preservation versus wealth maximization) is one notable reason for divergent opinions about sustainable development and economic globalization. Sustainable development and global free enterprise both seek to "preserve" or nurture capital in some sense, but their objectives differ. Many advocates of sustainable development seek to preserve natural capital, but also to preserve the native form, traditional uses, and physical integrity of natural capital. Many capitalists seek to "preserve" capital but also to expand wealth, and in so doing they engage often in the process of "creative destruction," the liquidation of capital in one form and the reinvestment of capital into other more productive forms. Indeed, a prevailing view of free enterprise (and free trade policy) is that capital should be free to be liquidated and to flow from one investment to another and from one country to another, which may contradict the objective of preserving natural capital.

If economic globalization fulfills its promise of increased global prosperity, then perhaps some accumulated wealth or surplus private capital may be invested in sustainable forest management, in conservation of natural biological diversity, or in helping to extend or preserve natural capital, such as through philanthropic or conservancy foundations, for example. Opportunities for such investments were explored in considerable detail in a recent report for the MacArthur Foundation (Best and Jenkins 1999). Evolving forms of equity ownership and diversified sources of forest revenue (non-timber products, recreation and eco-tourism, watershed services, and carbon sequestration credits) may offer a variety of new forest investment opportunities. However, timber revenue remains the primary revenue source for forestry in general, while preservation-oriented forestry may reduce timber revenues and require more capital to be tied up in forestland investments (particularly if it implies larger trees with longer rotations). By contrast, free trade and globalization impose few constraints on liquidity of private capital, and without constraints accumulated wealth or capital may be used for any purpose. In particular, accumulated wealth may be used for consumptive purposes, such buying new automobiles or new homes, rather than paying for wildlife sanctuaries, forest preserves, or sustainable forest management, while timber capital may be liquidated and invested in more profitable enterprises, such as real estate development, for example.

In the United States, government and forest industry have collaborated in sustainable forest management, but the industry has also liquidated forest investments. In May 2004, U.S. Secretary of Interior Gale Norton and International Paper Corporation signed the Aquatic Resources Conservation and Management Partnership Agreement, covering 5.5 million acres of International Paper forestlands in nine Southern states (PaperAge 2004). Under the agreement, U.S. Fish and Wildlife Service biologists provided technical assistance as International Paper conducted ecological surveys and conservation projects to help in recovery and re-introduction of aquatic species and restoration of habitat. The agreement also called for promoting public awareness of the needs for restoring imperiled species. However, in April 2006, International Paper announced the sale of most of its U.S. timberland holdings, 5.1 million acres of timberland for total proceeds of $6.1 billion.

The Montréal Process adopted the idea that free trade is itself an indicator of sustainable development. Montréal Process Indicators 58 and 59 (under Criterion 7) specifically outlined principles of free trade. Indicator 58 called for "investment and taxation policies and a regulatory environment . . . that permits the flow of capital in and out of the forest sector in response to market signals . . . in order to meet long-term demands for forest products and services," while Indicator 59 called for "nondiscriminatory trade policies for forest products." There is still a need, however, to explain how globalization and free trade affect sustainability and social welfare; for example, what happens to forests or forest-dependent communities when capital flows out of a local forest sector.

Issues of governance that are at the core of sustainable development may devolve ultimately to issues of governance pertaining to allocation of private capital, but rules of governance pertaining to allocation of private capital are not well established in free trade policy nor in conventions such as the Montréal Process Criteria and Indicators. Economic globalization may enhance private wealth and prosperity, but if prosperity does not translate into socially and environmentally sustainable development, then some scholars suggest that globalization may become subject to new political rules designed to ensure sustainable development. Just as new rules of governance were introduced in America in the late 19th and early 20th centuries to channel expansion of free enterprise and interstate commerce in a more socially responsible manner during America's industrialization and railroading era, some have speculated that new rules of governance may be needed to "civilize" the forces of economic globalization by channeling capital more in the direction of socially and environmentally sustainable development (Kates 2003).

In general, rules of governance concerning allocation of private capital are antithetical to ideals of free enterprise and free trade and are probably too complex as a matter of equity to arise as an adjunct to trade policies (which are usually focused on international rules of commerce, not governance of social or environmental equity). In the absence of rules of governance pertaining to sustainable development, the focus shifts to explaining how the forces of globalization, consolidation, and structural change are operating in the forest sector, creating a new and evolving context for sustainable forest management.

Globalization and Socioeconomic Benefits of Forest Management

This section discusses mainly effects on Montréal Process Criterion 6, which is the "maintenance and enhancement of long-term multiple socio-economic benefits to meet the needs of society." Criterion 6 is concerned with sustainability from an economic and social perspective, and in recent years economic globalization and structural change have affected economic and social sustainability in the U.S. forest sector.

Economic globalization and consolidation in the U.S. forest sector negatively impacted many economic benefits derived traditionally from forest management in the United States. Declining output of furniture negatively affected the output of higher grade hardwood lumber, while output of higher grades of softwood lumber and millwork were also displaced by imports. Along with declines in wood pulp output and pulpwood harvest, real pulpwood prices fell by about one-third from 1997 to 2002 (Fig. 20). The gross output of forestry in the United States likewise fell by 29% from 1995 to 2001, primarily reflecting nationwide trends in timber revenues and receipts (Fig. 21). The contribution of forestry to U.S. GDP declined along with the value and volume of domestic wood product output. Those declines largely reflect effects of economic globalization and structural changes in the forest sector.

Timberland investment appreciation also declined. For the first time in many years, the NCRIEF timberland index showed a decline in timberland value in 2000 and 2001, coincident with downturns in U.S. industrial output, declines in pulpwood demand and pulpwood prices, declines in output of higher grade hardwood lumber for furniture, declining wood panel exports, and declining output of softwood molding and millwork (NCRIEF 2006). The forest product industry divested millions of acres of timberland in recent years, partly because of tax and accounting rules, but also because of reduced raw material needs, higher imports, and the leveling out of timberland value appreciation.

Similarly, the opportunity for extension and use of new technology in forestry was eroded. Development of more productive silviculture systems, such as hybrid poplar plantations, was slowed or reversed as pulpwood demand receded.

The number of registered forestry professionals (members of SAF) declined over the past decade (by 15%), a decline that was reflected by a concurrent decline in nationwide timber receipts.

Forest product industry direct mill employment and earnings suffered substantial losses in recent years, both as a result of reductions in mill output and also as a result of more intense competition in secondary industries such as the furniture sector, with cost-cutting, downsizing, and automation. With the loss of higher wage forest industry jobs, local forest community economic viability and adaptability to change have also suffered.

The import share of forest product consumption increased significantly in recent years, as exports leveled out or declined. Import shares of the market in all major forest product sectors increased, including imports of wood panels, lumber, furniture, pulp and paper. With the loss of growth in U.S. manufacturing and industrial output, there was also a displacement of domestic demands for products such as corrugated containerboard used for packaging and shipping containers, or printing paper used for print advertising. The process of economic globalization and structural change entailed shifts in foreign versus local production, consumption, and supply of wood and wood products.

In general, the short-run influence of these trends on timber resource supply and demand was to offset growth in resource demand and reduce pressure on resource supply, leading to continued expansion in the nationwide volume of timber growing stock inventory and a relative abundance of timber supply (in the near term at least). In the long run, it remains to be seen whether the relative abundance of timber supply will persist. Rational expectations would suggest that managers of timberland may reduce management intensity (and in the long run timber output) in response to excess supply.

There are also various regional implications for forest management under economic circumstances where timber demand does not expand as rapidly as anticipated in the past, with the U.S. forest product industry exposed to more intense global competition. The regional implications can be understood by focusing on long-term effects on stumpage prices, land values, and returns to forest management in specific regions.

In the South, past forest management focused on development of pine plantations and management of Southern Pine (chiefly loblolly pine), which has become the mainstay of Southern forest industries. The recent glut in pine pulpwood prices resulted in diminished returns for silviculture activities such as management and thinning of pine plantations, while also reducing the rate of appreciation in timberland value. For the first time in modern history, the stumpage and delivered prices of pine pulpwood were lower in 2003 than hardwood pulpwood prices in the South. Softwood

saw timber demand remained relatively strong and balanced with supply, but maturing pine plantations will substantially increase supply of smaller saw logs within the next decade or two. Meanwhile, for hardwood saw timber and hardwood forests, erosion of demand for higher grade hardwood lumber and saw logs in the furniture sector has resulted in diminished revenues for landowners and logging contractors.

In the North, some contrast can be drawn between the effects of globalization in the Northeast and North Central (Lake States) regions. The Northeast has experienced higher than average declines in pulpwood demand, with closures of many smaller mills, while pulpwood demand has remained remarkably more even in the North Central region. However, with lackluster growth in pulp and paper and recent declines in furniture, little if any growth in timber demand is anticipated in the North.

In the West, particularly in interior regions, declining regional pulpwood demand, loss of OSB capacity, and loss of market share to imports for higher grades of clear softwood lumber (in molding and millwork) have left much of the interior with expanding timber inventories and few market incentives for tree thinning (small diameter timber removal) or timber stand improvement. Ironically, market incentives for thinning declined at the same time that needs increased for thinning to reduce fire hazard and restore forest health on millions of acres of public and private forestland in the interior West. Economic returns to forest management and economic feasibility of forest health restoration are thus challenged by limited markets for timber in the interior West.

Philosophical Implications for "Sustainability"

Observations in preceding sections of this report indicate that managing forests according to a "sustainability" paradigm (as in "sustainable forest management") will necessitate continuous adjustment to the economic, social, and ecological context of forest resource management, because that context continuously evolves and changes over time. In that sense, the philosophical concept of "sustainability" (economic, social, or ecological sustainability) is not unlike the concept of "economic feasibility"—both are concepts that evolve and change over time, with subjective evaluations that depend on context and circumstance. That which may appear to be sustainable (or economically feasible) at one point in time or in one context may not appear sustainable (or feasible) at a different point in time or another context, although there may be some consistency in measures by which outcomes are judged to be more or less sustainable.

In essence, the evolving economic, social, and ecological context of sustainable forest management reveals that sustainability can be approached philosophically only in a temporal sense through ordinal measures in the economic, social, and ecological dimensions. Like the concept of economic feasibility, measures that pertain to the concept of sustainability have a temporal aspect, evolving over time. Sustainability may be subject to ordinal ranking—measurable at points of time on an ordinal scale ranging from more to less—but there is never likely to be a cardinal measurement rule that will universally define sustainability for all time (the same being certainly true for the concept of economic feasibility).

The Montréal Process indicates that it is possible to obtain general agreement on ordinal measures or directional indicators of sustainability, just as there are generally accepted ordinal measures of economic feasibility (such as rate of return on investment, or net present value). Ordinal indicators may reveal, for example, whether different forest management approaches appear to be more or less sustainable, but developing a cardinal measure of sustainability in itself is as implausible as a cardinal measure of economic feasibility. It is unlikely therefore that absolute rules or cardinal measures will be developed by which to gauge performance in the realm of sustainability, although there are likely to be temporal measures on ordinal scales. The best that one can hope to do in measuring sustainability (as in the case of economic feasibility) is to continually study how the economic, social, and ecological context of sustainable forest management is evolving and changing over time.

This report provided some examples of that kind of study, looking at how economic globalization has influenced markets for forest products and timber in the United States. However, future development of sustainable forest management practices and strategies will require continuous future development of knowledge about the broader economic, social, and ecological context of sustainable forest management. As explained in the following section, intelligent discussion of potential responses to globalization and structural change goes far beyond conventional criteria and indicators of sustainable forest management (such as the Montréal Process Criteria and Indicators).

Potential Strategic Responses

This section discusses potential strategic responses that may be directed at relieving or coping with economic effects of globalization and structural change, by aiming to improve or maintain the competitiveness or competitive position of the U.S. forest sector. The following approaches were mentioned briefly in previous sections, and are followed by concise discussion of relative merits and shortcomings:

- Import duties, wage or benefit constraints, tax incentives, or subsidies

- Promotion of U.S. environmental and labor standards globally

- Trade liberalization

- Free currency exchange

- Increased automation, technological efficiency, and productivity

- Global enterprise development

- Product differentiation, standardization, and certification

- Advancing infrastructure, skills, and training

Import Duties, Wage or Benefit Constraints, Tax Incentives, or Subsidies

Historically tariffs, import duties, or other trade barriers were imposed in response to foreign competition. We can see a long history of negative experiences with protective trade barriers in general, such as the protraction of the Great Depression in the 1930s associated historically with the erection of protective trade barriers under the Smoot–Hawley Tariff Act of 1930. Consequently, although import duties and trade barriers still exist, free trade is favored institutionally (e.g., WTO) and by government policy. Special circumstances in some cases, such as evidence of foreign subsidies or dumping of products in select markets, may permit imposition of punitive tariffs in response to claims of injury from unfair import competition. The United States imposed in recent years countervailing and antidumping duties on softwood lumber imports from Canada, and in 2004 the United States imposed preliminary antidumping duties on wood furniture imports from China. However, tariffs and trade barriers in general are subject to review by the WTO and are limited under trade agreements such as NAFTA. Other undesirable ways to boost U.S. industry competitiveness might include constraints on wages or benefits for U.S. workers, compromising of natural resource conservation efforts, reductions in worker safety or health protection, exemption of industry from environmental protection standards, or targeted government subsidies or tax exemptions. However, such approaches are unlikely to gain broad political support for obvious reasons, or may be counterproductive in the long run. For example, Canadian softwood lumber producers invested in larger and more competitive sawmills to counterbalance import duties, and overall U.S. softwood lumber imports increased in the period when import duties were imposed. Subsidies or tax incentives for domestic industry can also lead to countervailing duties on U.S. exports.

Promotion of U.S. Environmental and Labor Standards Globally

In general, U.S. industry operates under the constraints of U.S. standards for worker health and safety, minimum wages, and environmental protection, which tend to be relatively higher and more costly than in some other regions of the world. The added cost burdens of employee benefits, pollution abatement, litigation costs, and added corporate tax burdens were estimated recently to provide an average foreign cost advantage of 18% relative to U.S. manufacturing costs, based on trade-weighted cost estimates for the nine leading U.S. trading partners (NAM 2003a). Thus, apart from reforming or reducing U.S. standards for worker health and safety or environmental protection, it would appear that another strategy to enhance U.S. industry cost competitiveness would be to achieve broader global acceptance of U.S. environmental and labor standards, so as to help level the playing field of international cost competition.

Both of the "inverted-U shaped" Kuznets curves—the classical Kuznets income-inequality curve and the "environmental Kuznets curve"—suggest that global acceptance of U.S. wage and labor standards as well as environmental protection standards may be advanced through simultaneous promotion of U.S. environmental and labor standards as well as higher wage standards on a global scale. In 1955, Simon Kuznets presented data that advanced the classical "Kuznets curve" hypothesis that income inequality first increases but then recedes with economic development, as a result of structural change (Kuznets 1955). More recently, that hypothesis was extended by data observations that support the so-called "environmental Kuznets curve" hypothesis that environmental effects of an economy also first increase but then later diminish with increasing per capita income (Stern 2004). Although there is some empirical evidence for Kuznets curves, the evidence is statistically weak, or has been challenged by other studies that reject the Kuznets hypotheses (particularly in the case of the Kuznets income-inequality curve).

Nevertheless, some basic observations can be made about environmental standards and income in relation to international competitiveness of the U.S. forest sector. The first observation, as noted previously, is that U.S. firms are placed at competitive disadvantage when competing against firms in countries that have much lower wages or less rigorous environmental standards. Indeed, it has been observed that when U.S. forest product firms are required to spend more on environmental protection than international competitors, it hurts U.S. forest industry competitiveness (Stern 2004; Ravallion and Chen 1997; Moore 2003).

Another basic observation is that people everywhere are likely to recognize that they benefit socially from higher wages and better safety, health, or environmental protection. Thus, regardless of whether evidence strongly supports the Kuznets curve hypotheses or not, it seems clear that there might be popular support for increased international acceptance of U.S. standards for worker health and safety protection and minimum wages, which in turn would benefit the competitiveness of U.S. industry (as well as potentially increase demand for U.S. exports). Furthermore, if there is any credibility to the environmental Kuznets curve hypotheses, then higher per-capita income in low-income countries should also help to raise expectations and elevate their standards for safety, health, and environmental protection.

Thus, one strategic approach to enhancing U.S. industry competitiveness might be to amplify Kuznets curves globally by promoting more rapid adoption of standards similar to U.S. standards for minimum wages, worker safety and health, and environmental protection. Wages in low-income countries may remain substantially lower than U.S. wages for generations to come, but promotion of U.S. standards abroad may influence expectations such that the Kuznets curves in low-income countries may become amplified or narrowed, as shown in Figure 50. In low-income countries, modest increases in income may suffice to reduce income disparity and provide substantial social benefits, and likewise modest increases in per-capita income may suffice to boost expectations and demands for safety, health, and environmental standards, which would help level the international playing field for U.S. manufacturers.

However, a drawback to this strategy is that workers and citizens in many low-income countries lack the same degree of representation in government or same degree of labor organization that has been enjoyed by U.S. citizens. Thus, even if promotion of U.S. standards for health, safety, minimum wages or environmental protection succeeded in gaining popular support in low-income countries, it is not certain that political institutions or circumstances in those countries would enable efficient adoption of such standards. Also, multinational corporations may oppose the adoption of laws that could boost labor standards or wages in countries like China (Barboza 2006).

Trade Liberalization

Liberalization of trade, chiefly through reduction of tariffs and removing barriers that inhibit free trade, as well as promotion of global free enterprise, is the more traditional policy approach to economic globalization. Under the auspices of the WTO and other international agreements, the United States and most other countries are committed to ideals of trade liberalization. Free trade and free enterprise have potential to expand global wealth and prosperity by allocating capital resources to the most productive and efficient investments worldwide, while contributing to ongoing expansion of global interconnectedness in society and culture. Trade liberalization can still work in favor of U.S. producers; for example, U.S. producers of paper and paperboard were exposed recently to threats of increased tariffs on imports of their products in the European Union (in retaliation to U.S. export tax incentives and also customs duties on U.S. steel imports). In 2004, the Chinese government extended for 5 years antidumping duties on newsprint imports from the United States and other countries. A less obvious but significant barrier to free enterprise is government-subsidized capacity expansion in some foreign countries. Although imports have surged over the past decade, U.S. exports have also increased, and the United States still exports millions of tons of products such as pulp and paper each year (Fig. 48). Thus, trade liberalization is still an important means of expanding markets and enhancing economic opportunities for U.S. manufacturers.

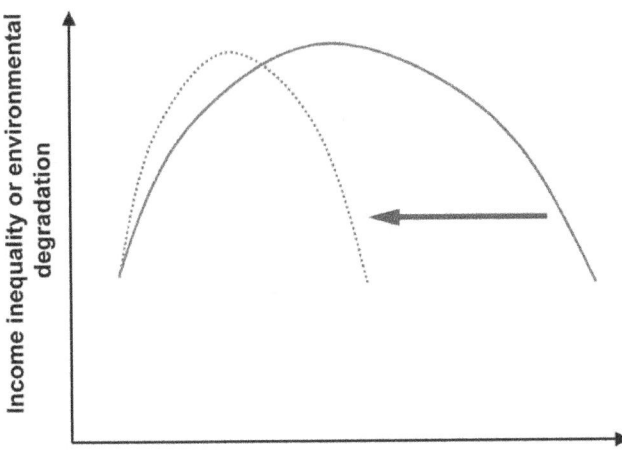

Figure 50—Stylized illustration of amplified Kuznets curve.

Free Currency Exchange

Deregulated exchange of currency as an adjunct to free trade policy may also help provide some relief from effects of economic globalization. The rise of imports and outsourcing of U.S. production were boosted in recent years by artificially low currency exchange rates or officially regulated currency exchange at rates lower than real purchasing power of foreign currencies in some low-income countries. The effect of fixed exchange rates was compounded by maintaining low exchange rates for extended periods in developing countries undergoing rapid economic expansion and shifts in the purchasing power of their currencies. The effect was to create artificially low dollar-denominated wages in those countries, enhancing their real cost competitiveness relative to U.S. manufacturers while inhibiting their purchases of U.S. goods. The People's Republic of China is a prime example. China fixed the dollar exchange rate at a low level for many years (at 12.1¢ per yuan), preserving low dollar-denominated wages in China despite enormous economic expansion and growth. Low wages attracted massive capital investment, particularly investment in capacity to produce goods sold to the United States. The United States experienced consequently enormous trade deficits with China ($124 billion in 2003). However, instability was introduced to the Chinese banking sector as a direct result of pegging the Chinese currency value to the value of the U.S. dollar as it declined from 2002 to 2004 (Bremner and others 2004). China also began to experience a global trade deficit ($8.4 billion by the first quarter of 2004) as it continued to expand imports of raw materials to feed its rapid economic expansion. Consequently, China has begun to loosen constraints on official exchange rates.

Still other developing countries have maintained low currency exchange rates despite economic expansion, favoring trade surpluses in goods with the United States but also contributing to economic instability as the dollar fluctuates in value. While the WTO enforces global commitments to free trade, the IMF administers rules pertaining to fixing or manipulation of currency exchange. Through diplomacy and IMF channels, the United States may have an opportunity to obtain more liberalized currency exchange rates as an adjunct to trade liberalization. Without free currency exchange, many benefits of trade liberalization may continue flowing mainly in a one-way direction from the United States to other countries, and particularly to low-income countries with artificially low exchange rates, creating imbalanced trade flows, economic instability, and imbalanced opportunities for forest sector development.

Automation, Efficiency, and Productivity

The strategy of increased automation, technological efficiency, and productivity gain is commonly employed in the forest product industry (and elsewhere in manufacturing) to cope with import competition, excess capacity, and low profits. That strategy was facilitated in recent years by advances in production technology through computer control and automation of production processes, adoption of new information technologies, and more efficient distribution systems. These and other advances along with pressures to reduce costs and increase profits contributed to a significantly higher rate of labor displacement in U.S. manufacturing over the past decade. While gains in productivity contributed to survival of more automated and capital-intensive firms in the U.S. forest sector, gains in productivity were achieved also in other countries through capital investment.

Competing firms in countries such as Canada, for example, invested heavily in forest product industry productivity, in sawmills and OSB mills, and earlier in furniture plants. Capital investment increased more recently in countries with lower wage rates such as in China, with new furniture plants and large new paper mills. Thus, the strategy of increased automation, technological efficiency, and productivity gain with larger and more capital-intensive production facilities is a necessary strategy in maintaining industry competitiveness, but that strategy is not the sole prerogative of U.S. producers and also therefore not solely sufficient as a panacea for the U.S. forest sector.

Global Enterprise Development

Global enterprise development is yet another strategic approach taken by some firms in the forest product sector, most notably by Scandinavian pulp and paper firms who have expanded globally over the past decade and also by some U.S. furniture producers who have shifted production capacity abroad. As capital flows unimpeded across national borders, opportunities for global enterprise development have expanded. Competitive economic efficiencies can be achieved by outsourcing production to low-income countries, and those efficiency gains may make global enterprise development imperative for financial success. Innovations in electronic communication, computing, and product distribution also accelerate design, production, and delivery of goods, such that improved production processes and opportunities for market development are spreading throughout the world. The shifting of wood furniture production capacity and outsourcing of wood furniture components to production facilities in low-income countries is a prime example of that trend, with foreign producers or foreign subsidiaries gaining ability to participate in development of custom or niche furniture markets, sometimes just as readily or effectively as local producers (evidenced by significant expansion in the import share of the U.S. wood furniture market). United States firms that develop international operations and pursue global enterprise development can participate also in reaping the benefits of economic globalization. However, as forest sector production capacity and technology move offshore, so do growth in employment and growth in domestic timber markets, with negative effects on the ability to maintain socioeconomic benefits of sustainable forest management.

Product Differentiation and Certification

Although many forest products are sold in mass commodity markets, such as commodity grades of lumber, wood panels, or paper and paperboard, there are some avenues to expand revenues by product differentiation, via product specialization, voluntary standardization, or product certification. One common business strategy is to seek development of niche markets, but that strategy also entails the difficulty of specialized marketing research and development of specialty products. Globally interconnected markets also demand increasingly uniform product quality, and are intolerant toward inferior quality or local variation in product quality. The engineering standardization of forest products via ASTM International (originally known as the American Society for Testing and Materials or ASTM), ISO (International Organization for Standardization), and various means of engineering certification of products permit producers who achieve a high degree of product standardization or product certification to differentiate their product in increasingly competitive global markets. However, ensuring product compliance with engineering standards or performance certification requires ability to produce products with uniform quality control. In general, better quality control and improved product quality depend on capital investment, affording more automation and engineering quality control in manufacturing and generally favoring modern capital-intensive production facilities.

In some cases, forest product producers may also obtain environmental certification of products or name branding that differentiates their products from other similar products or other competing materials in the marketplace. Forest products may be recognized in the market for environmental performance such as lower energy input or less use of nonrenewable resources relative to other materials such as metals or plastics (provided that appropriate product life-cycle assessment studies support claims of such advantages), but better environmental performance also requires modernization and capital investments. Product differentiation through

certification and name branding will remain an important competitive element of forest product marketing and development, both within the United States and abroad, primarily under voluntary standardization and certification initiatives.

Advancing Infrastructure, Skills, and Training

Last, a broader and longer-range strategic approach is advancement of the infrastructure, skills, and training needed to enhance global competitiveness and success of U.S. firms in the forest product sector. This strategic option includes development of forest resources for the future, research and development of future forest products and technologies, and providing education, training, and skills for the forest sector workforce of the future.

In previously unexpected ways, globalization, consolidation, and structural change have influenced future needs for resources, infrastructure, skills, and training. Projected timber harvest in the United States is lower in the most recent RPA timber assessment than in previous timber assessments, largely because of lower projected pulpwood demand as a result of economic globalization and increased paper recycling in the pulp and paper sector. Projected future growth in timber demand is likely to be met primarily by expanded output of wood fiber from managed plantations, primarily Southern Pine plantations, although slower growth in demand and lower pulpwood prices raise questions about future investment in plantation establishment and growth. The forest industry has divested millions of acres of commercial timberland in recent years, and capital investment within the U.S. pulp and paper industry has declined.

Nevertheless, because of increased automation and the shift throughout manufacturing toward more capital- or skill-intensive enterprises, improved skills and training are needed now more than ever before. However, declining employment trends in U.S. manufacturing and in forest products tend to reduce incentives for workers to pursue careers in manufacturing or forest products, while the U.S. demographic distribution limits the number of younger U.S. workers entering the workforce (Fig. 25). According to the National Science Foundation, foreign students accounted for most of the growth in U.S. science and engineering doctorates since the late 1980s, and foreign students accounted for more than half (56%) of all U.S. engineering doctorates awarded in 2001 (NSF 2004). Clearly the U.S. forest sector faces challenges in developing resource and technology infrastructure as well as worker skills and training needed to restore and maintain global competitiveness and growth. Challenges faced by U.S. manufacturers in developing the workforce of the future are discussed in more detail in a recent report by the National Association of Manufacturers (2003b).

Summary

Various approaches can be taken in seeking to relieve or cope with effects of economic globalization and structural change in the U.S. forest sector. Eight different categories of strategic approaches were identified that might be aimed at sustaining the global competitiveness of the U.S. forest sector, including (1) import duties, wage or benefit constraints, tax incentives or subsidies, (2) promotion of U.S. environmental and labor standards globally, (3) trade liberalization, (4) free currency exchange, (5) automation, efficiency and productivity gains, (6) global enterprise development, (7) product differentiation and certification, and (8) advancement of the resource and technology infrastructure as well as training and skills needed for future sustainable forest sector development. All these approaches have limitations or drawbacks. Without more detailed analysis of these approaches, there is little basis for speculation about their effects on the competitiveness of the U.S. forest sector, and it would be misleading to suggest that any particular approach is recommended. However, a mix of these approaches is already being pursued to some extent. Thus, understanding consequences of globalization and structural change for sustainable forest management will require monitoring and evaluating a spectrum of behavioral responses and forest management options that will unfold in the evolving context of forest sector globalization, consolidation and structural change.

Conclusions

Economic globalization deeply impacted the U.S. forest sector in recent years and reshaped opportunities for sustainable forest management in the United States. Globalization accelerated structural changes in the overall economy and in U.S. forest product markets. Increased imports of goods stimulated capacity expansion abroad and led to a period of overcapacity, reduced profits, and consolidation in manufacturing and in various forest product industries. The forest sector has been historically subject to competition, but trade liberalization and economic globalization led to expanded import competition from low-cost foreign competitors. Thus, since the early 1990s globalization and import competition appear to have had rather profound effects on trends in the U.S. forest sector. After increasing for much of the previous century, U.S. output of products such as wood pulp and wood furniture peaked in the mid to late 1990s and then declined for a number of years along with overall U.S. industrial output.

Economic globalization and import competition favored survival of enterprises in the United States that were more capital-intensive, skill-intensive, or generally more automated and technologically advanced. Although imports gained market share for all principal categories of forest products, the domestically produced share of U.S. consumption remained higher for the more capital-intensive industries such as pulp and paper and structural wood panels, while falling to lower levels for less capital-intensive or more labor-intensive industries such as sawmills and furniture plants. Average capacities of U.S. lumber mills, wood panel mills, pulp mills, and paper mills all increased

even though the numbers of mills declined, as smaller less efficient mills were closed. Global markets and global enterprise developments, rather than local or regional developments, as in the past, increasingly influence U.S timber markets.

Globalization and ongoing structural changes affected also the opportunities for sustainable forest management in the United States. Observable changes that appear to have resulted from globalization and structural change include declines in the economic value of forestry outputs, forest sector employment, economic feasibility of forest management, and gross contribution of forestry to GDP. Economic globalization and the trade deficit have also made the U.S. housing sector increasingly dependent on foreign purchases of U.S. financial assets. Such changes in timber markets can alter economic, social, and environmental dimensions of forest management, suggesting that more in-depth strategic monitoring and analysis of the issue is warranted in planning sustainable forest management policies for the future with careful consideration of strategies to cope with realities and challenges of economic globalization and structural change.

Finally, changes in the economic, social, and environmental dimensions of forest management have led to notable adjustments in the outlook for sustainable forest management in the United States. Traditionally, foresters and forest resource professionals in the United States were accustomed to escalating demands for timber, resulting in a traditional focus on timber management and productivity. That focus will certainly not disappear, but the phenomena of globalization, overcapacity, and the excess of timber growth over demand (across the northern hemisphere at least) will likely cause some shift in future forestry priorities and opportunities in the United States.

From a broad perspective, the trends suggest greater challenges for sustainable forest management in the following areas:

- Promoting the broad relevance of local sustainable forest management activity in a context of global cost-cutting, efficiency imperatives, and shifts in capital flows

- Managing small-diameter timber with limited growth in local market demand

- Defining the future role of forestry technology development in general

- Matching forestry priorities to evolving socioeconomic needs

Managing forests according to a "sustainability" paradigm (as in "sustainable forest management") will necessitate continuous study of the economic, social, and ecological context of forest management, as that context continuously evolves and changes over time. Some topics specifically related to economic globalization and the forest sector, which warrant further analysis or more in-depth research, include the following:

- Consequences of disconnect between resource demand and GDP growth

  How will the connection between forest resource demand growth and U.S. GDP evolve, and what will determine future trends in forest resource demand? Also, how will U.S. housing demand evolve in the context of economic globalization?

- Divergence in global competitiveness and growth among global regions

  What factors will determine global forest sector competitiveness and growth, and how will the forest sector evolve competitively in the future, given the demand potential of China, supply potential of Russia, and other emerging markets?

- Exchange rate determinacy and policy effects

  Given the large influence of real exchange rates on trade and growth in the U.S. forest sector, what are the implications of alternative currency exchange policies?

- Effects of expanded global wood fiber plantations and recycled fiber

  How will the shift toward productive wood fiber plantations or use of recycled fiber (trends which have also reduced harvest pressures on natural forests) evolve over the long run in the context of economic globalization?

- Long-run effect of economic globalization on sustainable forest management

  In the long run, will the drivers of economic globalization (profitability, market development, cost competitiveness, and economic efficiency) subordinate less productive objectives of sustainable forest resource management (e.g., social or environmental objectives)? Or, will those drivers contribute toward greater overall wealth and prosperity such that society will better afford to meet those objectives of sustainable forest management? Meanwhile, how will forestry be funded in a context of slower growth in demand for forest products?

References

AF&PA. 2002. 44th Annual capacity report press release. Washington, D.C.: American Forest & Paper Association. http://www.afandpa.org/Content/NavigationMenu/Pulp_ and Paper/Statistics Publications1/44th Annual Capacity_Report_Press_Release.htm

AF&PA. 2003. Statistics of paper, paperboard & wood pulp. Washington, D.C.: American Forest & Paper Association. www.afandpa.org/

AF&PA. 2006. Paper, paperboard and wood pulp monthly statistical summary. Washington, D.C.: American Forest and Paper Association. Vol. 84, No. 7 (and earlier issues).

APA. 2003. RISI world wood product study. Wood Based Panels International. Tacoma, WA: APA – The Engineered Wood Association.

APA. 2006a. Economic report E172, structural panel and engineered wood yearbook. Tacoma, WA: APA – The Engineered Wood Association.

APA. 2006b. Market outlook, March 2006. Tacoma, WA: APA – The Engineered Wood Association.

APA. 2006c. Regional production and market outlook. Publication E72. Prepared by Craig Adair. Tacoma, WA: APA – The Engineered Wood Association.

ASM. 2006. Annual survey of manufacturers. Washington, D.C.: U.S. Census Bureau. www.census.gov/mcd/asmhome.html

Banister, J. 2005. Manufacturing earnings and compensation in China. Monthly Labor Review 128(8):22–40.

Barboza, D. 2006. China drafts law to boost unions and end abuse. New York Times. October 13, 2006. Front page.

Bazdarich, M.; Thornberg, C.F. 2004. The labor market is different this time: you should know how and why. UCLA Anderson Forecast: White Paper Series. www.anderson.ucla.edu/research/forecast/forecast/2004/insights/ai labor-markets 0404 1.pdf

BEA. 2002. Gross output by detailed industry, 1977–2001. NDN-0303. Washington, D.C.: U.S. Department of Commerce Bureau of Economic Analysis.

BEA. 2004. GDP by industry report (NDN-0303). Washington, D.C.: U.S. Department of Commerce Bureau of Economic Analysis. www.bea.doc.gov/bea/uguide.htm# 1 14

Bernard, B.; Jensen, J.B.; Schott, P.K. 2002. Survival of the best fit: competition from low wage countries and the (uneven) growth of U.S. manufacturing plants. Yale School of Management Working Paper No. ES-21; Tuck School of Business Working Paper No. 02-17.

Best, C.; Jenkins, M. 1999. Opportunities for investment—capital markets and sustainable forestry. Boonville, CA: Pacific Forest Trust, Inc., and John D. and Catherine T. MacArthur Foundation. 80 p.

BLS. 2006a. Washington, D.C.: U.S. Department of Labor Bureau of Labor Statistics. www.bls.gov/data/home htm

BLS. 2006b. Washington, D.C.: U.S. Department of Labor Bureau of Labor Statistics. http://stats.bls.gov/bls/international htm

Bremner, B.; Roberts, D.; Balfour, F. (With Bruce Einhorn in Shenzhen and bureau reports). 2004. Business Week. China: headed for a crisis? (International cover story). May 3, 2004. www.businessweek.com/magazine/content/04 18/b3881012.htm

Census Bureau. 2002a. Annual capital expenditures survey. Washington, D.C.: U.S. Department of Commerce, Census Bureau, Economics and Statistics Administration. ACE/02 (and earlier editions). 18 p. plus appendices. www.census.gov/csd/ace/pubs html

Census Bureau. 2002b. 2002 Economic census, industry series. Washington, D.C.: U.S. Department of Commerce Census Bureau. www.census.gov/econ/census02/guide/IN-DRPT31 htm

Census Bureau. 2006a. Foreign trade statistics. Historical Series—U.S. International Trade in Goods. Washington, D.C.: U.S. Department of Commerce Census Bureau. www.census.gov/foreign-trade/statistics/historical/index html

Census Bureau. 2006b. Population projections. Washington, D.C.: U.S. Department of Commerce Census Bureau Population Division, Population Projections Branch. www.census.gov/population/www/projections/natdet.html

Chang, S.J. 1998. A generalized Faustmann model for the determination of the optimal harvest age. Canadian Journal of Forest Research 48(5):652–659.

Chinafacturing Solutions. 2006. Wage rates in China. www.chinafacturing.com/whychina html

CIA. 2006. World factbook. Country profile for China. Washington, D.C.: U.S. Central Intelligence Agency. www.cia.gov/cia/publications/factbook/index.html

Earth Summit. 1992. Non-legally binding authoritative statement of principles for a global consensus on the management, conservation and sustainable development of all types of forests. http://habitat.igc.org/agenda21/forest html

Economagic. 2006. Economic time series page. www.economagic.com/

Erb, G. 2001. Big trees take a fall—Many sawmills pay more for smaller logs. Puget Sound Business Journal. November 2, 2001.

Erlich, P.; Holdren, J. 1972. Review of the closing circle. Environment 14(3):24–39.

FAO. 1998. Global forest products outlook study. Rome, Italy: Food and Agriculture Organization of the United Nations. www fao.org/DOCREP/003/X1607E/X1607E00 htm

FAO. 2001. Global forest resources assessment 2000. FAO Forestry Paper 140. Rome, Italy: Food and Agriculture Organization of the United Nations.

www fao.org/forestry/foris/webview/forestry2/index.jsp?siteId=2921&sitetreeId=7947&langId=1&geoId=0

FAS. 2003. GAIN Report CH3118. Washington, D.C.: U.S. Department of Agriculture Foreign Agricultural Service.

FAS. 2006. Washington, D.C.: U.S. Department of Agriculture Foreign Agricultural Service. www fas.usda.gov/us-trade/USTExFAS.asp?QI=

Federal Reserve. 2006a. G.17 Industrial production and capacity utilization. Industrial production index, not seasonally adjusted (Historical monthly series). www.federalreserve.gov/releases/g17/table1_2.htm

Federal Reserve. 2006b. Open market operations. www federalreserve.gov/fomc/fundsrate.htm

Fedkiw, J. 1997. Managing multiple uses on national forests, 1905–1995. A 90-year learning experience and it isn't finished yet. Pub. FS-628. Washington, D.C.: USDA Forest Service. 284 p.

Fosgate, H. 2002. Timberland on the block . . . amid forest company mergers, takeovers. The Forester's Log. Warnell School of Forest Resources, University of Georgia. Spring 2002:13,15. www.forestry.uga.edu/h/alumni/flog/pdf/logS02.pdf#search=%22Clutter%20timberland%2014%20million%20acres%22

FRA. 2003. Annual pulpwood statistics summary report 1998–2002 (Pulpwood receipts data). Rockville, MD: Forest Resources Association. www.forestresources.org

Freddie Mac. 2006. 30-year fixed-rate mortgages Since 1971. Monthly average commitment rates for 30-year mortgage. www.freddiemac.com/pmms/pmms30 htm

FS. 2003. National report on sustainable forests–2003. FS-766. February, 2004. Washington, D.C.: U.S. Department of Agriculture, Forest Service. 139 p.

Hamilton, Gordon. 2004. Canfor feels comfortable. Vancouver Sun newspaper. May 1, 2004.

Hardwood Market Report. 2005: The year at a glance (special issue). Memphis, TN: Hardwood Market Report.

Hardwood Review. 2004. 2004 Annual forecast. Charlotte, NC: Hardwood Publishing Company.

Haynes, R.W. (coord.). 1990. An analysis of the timber situation in the United States: 1952 to 2040. Fort Collins, CO: USDA Forest Service. Rocky Mountain Forest and Range Experiment Station. General Technical Report RM-199. 268 p.

Haynes, R.W. (coord.). 2003. An analysis of the timber situation in the United States: 1952 to 2050. Portland, OR: USDA Forest Service. Pacific Northwest Experiment Station. PNW-GTR-560. 254 p. www.fs.fed.us/pnw/pubs/gtr560/

Haynes, R.W.; Adams, D.M.; Alig, R.J.; Ince, P.J.; Mills, J.R.; Zhou, X. 2006. The 2005 RPA timber assessment update. Gen. Tech. Rep. PNW-GTR-699. A technical document supporting the 2000 USDA Forest Service RPA assessment. Portland, OR: U.S. Department of Agriculture, Forest Service, Pacific Northwest Research Station.

Held, D.; McGrew, A.; Goldblatt, D.; Perraton, J. 1999. Global transformations: politics, economics, and culture. Stanford, CA: Stanford Press.

Howard, J.L. 2003a. U.S. timber production, trade, consumption and price statistics. USDA Forest Service. Madison, WI: Forest Products Laboratory. Research Paper FPL–RP–595. 90 p.

Howard 2003b. U.S. timber production, trade, consumption and price statistics, 1965–2002. Forest Products Laboratory, Madison, WI: USDA Forest Service. Research Paper FPL–RP–615. 90 p.

ITA. 2006. Washington, D.C.: International Trade Administration. Consumer Goods Division. www.ita.doc.gov/td/ocg/

ITC. 2004. U.S. Washington, D.C.: International Trade Commission. http://dataweb.usitc.gov/

Kant, S.S. 2004. Economics of sustainable forest management (editorial). Forest Policy and Economics. Elsevier 6(3):197–203.

Kates, R. 2003. The nexus and the neem tree: globalization and a transition toward sustainability (Chapter 6). In: Worlds apart: globalization and the environment. Washington D.C.: Island Press.

Kinstrey, R. 2004. Invest to improve: North America struggles to maintain its global cost competitiveness. Pulp and Paper, January, 2004:34–38.

Kuznets, S. 1955. Economic growth and income inequality. American Economic Review. 45(1):1–28.

Lackey, R. 2003. A salmon-centric view of the 21st century in the Western United States. In: Proceedings of the conference World Summit on Salmon, Simon Fraser University, June 10–13, Vancouver, British Columbia. Corvallis, OR: National Health and Environmental Effects Research Laboratory, U.S. Environmental Protection Agency.

Lardy, Nicholas R. 2003. United States–China ties: reassessing the economic relationship. Hearing of the House Committee on International Relations. October 21, 2003. wwwc.house.gov/international_relations/108/lard1021.htm

Luppold, William. 2006. USDA Forest Service. Data adapted from current industrial reports, U.S. Census Bureau, MA321T–Lumber Production and Mill Stocks. www.census.gov/cir/www/321/ma321t html#

Mann, Armistead & Epperson, Ltd. 2006. Investment Bankers, Richmond, VA. www.maeltd.com/

Mattoon, A.T. 1998. Paper Forests. World-Watch. March/April 1998:20–28.

Minor, Elliott. 2002. Planting programs of the 1980s may lead to tree glut. Savannah Morning News, September 15, 2002. Associated Press. http://savannahnow.com/stories/091502/LOCtreeglut.shtml

Montréal Process Working Group. 1998–2005. www.mpci.org/

Moore, W.H. 2003. Manufacturing vital to economic recovery. Comment in: Pulp & Paper 77:10.

NAM. 2003a. How structural costs imposed on U.S. manufacturers harm workers and threaten competitiveness. Washington, D.C.: Manufacturing Institute of the National Association of Manufacturers. 24 p. www.nam.org/s nam/sec.asp?CID=201308&DID=229450

NAM. 2003b. Keeping America competitive–How a talent shortage threatens U.S. manufacturing. Washington, D.C.: National Association of Manufacturers. 30 p. www.nam.org

NCREIF. 2006. NCREIF timberland index. Chicago, IL: National Council of Real Estate Investment Fiduciaries. www.ncreif.com/

Nimon, R.; Wesley, J.C.; Smith, M. 2002. NAFTA, agricultural trade, and the environment. In: Zahniser, S.; Link, J. (Editors). Effects of North American Free Trade Agreement on agriculture and the rural economy. USDA Economics Research Service (ERS) Agriculture and Trade Report No. WRS0201. 134 p.

NLK. 2002. Market pulp cost analysis. Vancouver, British Columbia: NLK Consultants, Inc.

NSF. 2004. Science and engineering indicators 2004. Arlington, Virginia: National Science Board of the National Science Foundation. www.nsf.gov/sbe/srs/seind04/

Nussbaum, Bruce. 2004. Special report—where are the jobs? Business Week, March 22, 2004. www.businessweek.com/magazine/content/04 12/b3875601 htm

PaperAge. 2004. International Paper, U.S. Interior Department sign environmental pact. May 27, 2004. www.paperage.com/2004news/05 27 2004ip.html

Paperloop. 2002. Mill managers survey. Pulp & Paper magazine 76(12):26.

Paperloop. 2004. Global fact & price book. Paperloop Publications (now RISI): Bedford, MA. 311 p.

Poyry, J. 1999. Global outlook for plantations. Research Report 99.9. Canberra, Australia: ABARE.

PPI. 2002. Pulp and Paper International fact and price book. Brussels, Belgium: Paperloop. 498 p.

Random Lengths (weekly report). 2006. Vol. 62 (and earlier issues). Eugene, OR: Random Lengths Publications. www.randomlengths.com

Ravallion M.; Chen, S. 1997. What can new survey data tell us about recent changes in distribution and poverty? World Bank Economic Review 11(2):357–82.

RISI. 2003. North American wood panels and EWP capacity report. Bedford, MA: Resource Information Systems.

RISI. 2004a. North American Wood Panels Forecast, December 2004 4(4). Bedford, MA: Resource Information Systems.

RISI. 2004b. PaperTree letter. Bedford, MA: Resource Information Systems. www.risiinfo.com/risi-store/do/home

RPA. 1989. USDA Forest Service. RPA Assessment of the forest and rangeland situation in the United States, 1989. Forest Resource Report 26. Washington, D.C.: U.S. Department of Agriculture. 72 p.

RPA. 2001. USDA Forest Service. 2000 RPA Assessment of forest and range lands. FS-687. Washington, D.C.: USDA Forest Service. 78 p.

Siry, J.; Bailey, R. 2003. Increasing southern pine growth and its implications for regional wood supply. Forest Products Journal 53(1):32–37.

Siry, J.; Cubbage, F.W.; Ahmed, M.R. 2003. Sustainable forest management: global trends and opportunities. 11 p. Accepted for publication in Journal of Forest Policy and Economics. www.sciencedirect.com

Smith, R.; Rice, R.W.; Ince, P.J. 2003. Pulp capacity in the United States, 2000. Gen. Tech. Rep. FPL–GTR–139. Madison, WI: U.S. Department of Agriculture, Forest Service, Forest Products Laboratory. 23 p.

Spelter, H.; Alderman, M. 2003. Profile 2003: Softwood sawmills in the United States and Canada. Res. Pap. FPL–RP–608. Madison, WI: U.S. Department of Agriculture, Forest Service, Forest Products Laboratory. 79 p.

Speth, J. 2003. Worlds apart: globalization and the environment. Washington D.C.: Island Press (p. 12).

Stern, D.I. 2004. Environmental Kuznets curve. In: Encyclopedia of Energy, Volume 3. Burlington, MA: Elsevier Academic Press.

Sum, A; Khatiwada, I.; Harrington, P.; Palma, S. 2003. New immigrants in the labor force and the number of employed new immigrants in the U.S. from 2000 to 2003: Continued growth amidst declining employment among the native born population. Boston, MA: Center for Labor Market Studies, Northeastern University. 20 p. www.nupr.neu.edu/01-04/immigration jan.pdf

Taylor, R.E. 2002. Wood Markets (monthly international solid wood report). February.

Tice, W. 2004. Canfor's Houston mill emphasizes production volume and cost efficiencies. Timber Processing Journal (reproduced from Canadian Wood Products), September. www.panelworldmag.com/vserver/hb/display.cfm?MagazineKey=5&IssueKey=459&SectionKey=273&ArticleKey=4327

Timber Mart South. 2006. www.tmart-south.com/tmart/prices.html

Tucker, B.M. 1984. Samuel Slater and the origins of the American textile industry, 1790–1860. Ithaca, NY: Cornell University Press.

UN. 2002. Report of the World Summit on Sustainable Development. Johannesburg, South Africa, 26 August–September 2002. A/CONF.199/20. New York: United Nations. 167 p. www.un.org/esa/sustdev/publications/publications.htm

UN. 2006. United Nations Department of Economic and Social Affairs, Division for Sustainable Development. www.un.org/esa/sustdev/

USDA Forest Service. 2007. Interim Update of the 2000 RPA Assessment of Forest and Range Lands. FS-875. Washington, DC.

U.S. Department of Commerce. 2004. Manufacturing in America: A comprehensive strategy to address the challenges to U.S. manufacturing. Washington, D.C. 88 p. (p. 9).

U.S. Department of Commerce. 2005. Quarterly financial report (QFR). www.census.gov/csd/qfr/

U.S. Department of the Treasury. 2006. Treasury International Capital System. www.treas.gov/tic/ticsec2.shtml

Victor, D.G. 2003. Forest plantations and a vision for restoring the forests. Keynote presentation at: UNFF experts meeting on the role of planted forests in sustainable forest management, 24–30 March 2003, New Zealand. www maf.govt nz/mafnet/unff-planted-forestry-meeting/conference-papers/

Victor, D.G.; Ausubel, J.H. 2000. Restoring the forests. Foreign Affairs 79(6): 127–144. http://greatrestoration rockefeller.edu/

Wagner, E.; Hanson, E. 2004. Ahead of the game: innovation and competitiveness in the U.S. wood products industry. Engineered Wood Journal. Spring 2004:23–25.

Wang, S. 2004. One hundred faces of sustainable forest management. Forest Policy and Economics. Elsevier (6):205–213.

Warren, Debra D. 2005. Production, prices, employment, and trade in Northwest forest industries, all quarters of

2003. Resource Bulletin. PNW–RB–247. Portland, OR: U.S. Department of Agriculture, Forest Service, Pacific Northwest Research Station. 171 p.

Wood Based Panels International. 2005. No. 1 February/ March 2005. Sidcup, UK: Polygon Media. p. 12–14 (OSB, North America); 16–18, 20, 22 (OSB, rest of the world).

Wood Markets. 2004. June/July, Vol. 9, No. 5. Vancouver, British Columbia: International Wood Markets Research, Inc. www.woodmarkets.com/

World Bank. 1999. Greening industry: new rules for communities, markets, and governments. A World Bank Policy Research Report. New York: Oxford University Press.

World Commission on Environment and Development. 1987. Our common future. Oxford: Oxford University Press. p. 8.

WRI. 2004. Wood resource quarterly. 3Q/2004. Bothell, WA: Wood Resources International, LLC. www.wri-ltd.com/

WTCA. 2002. Structural building components. Madison, WI: Wood Truss Council of America. www.sbcindustry. com/

WWPA. 2004. 2003 Statistical yearbook of the western lumber industry. Portland, OR: Western Wood Products Association.